I have watched Dan Hammer for a decade. I have seen him become a great leader. H(this text. This book offers practical wisdom/application (orthopraxis) and reflects a deep not material you race through. It calls you to reflect on leadership issues carefully. It is con

I believe we are all leaders. We all influence others. Some are innately fine leaders. Some become great leaders. I am honored to call Dan Hammer a friend and colleague. I am indebted to him for teaching me, through example, what it means to be a godly servant leader. I believe all will benefit from this book!

Rev. Dr. John Roddam
Rector: St. Luke's, Seattle

I have for a very long time loved the teaching of servant leadership but have at times been concerned at a tendency for it to be mis-interpreted as being a weaker form of leadership. Dan's portrayal is confident in correcting any possibility of that and creating a strong thesis that servant leadership is the strongest form of leadership, deriving its strength from God like character and purposes. This book is full of so many rich threads, covering every aspect and motivation of and for leadership. Dan's quote that this is not something we do for God, but rather something we do with God sets the tone for the entire book, lifting our eyes above an earthly labor to a heaven directed co-laboring. Read it and accept your leadership assignment and all that is needed to lead with Christ. The world is literally waiting to be led as Christ intended and equipped us for.

Paul Manwaring
Bethel Church, Redding, California

It has been my privilege to know Dan Hammer as a friend and to co-labor with him in the Seattle area in conference and training settings. I am familiar with the work of SonRise and Dan's style of leadership.

He is an exemplary Father figure, a Barnabas type of encourager and a gifted servant leader. Dan gives the outward appearance of a man who is happy to follow Jesus in the day to day and who is always amazed at the favor of God. Behind all of that there is also a very intentional man who is excellent at mentoring, affirming and developing the people whom God puts in his way.

Dan is a thinker and a strategist and combines that with an affectionate heart and a kind touch. Dan embraces people where they are and has every intention to see them become more of who they should be. It is entirely fitting that he should produce a workbook on Servant Leadership. He models it in his own heart and has the instincts of one who is himself an intimate of the Father.

As you will see in the book, Dan is a student of Leadership; a researcher of methodologies; and a practical exponent of principles leading to outcomes. This project is incarnational because that is Dan's style. He is deeply authentic in who he is and what he models. Prepare to be impacted greatly!

Graham Cooke
Author and Speaker, Dan Hammer's Friend

Dan Hammer has been my pastor for many years and during that time, I have watched him weather both the storms and the joys of leadership. A man of integrity, honor, and vision, his heart is to equip and release others as servant leaders in the body of Christ. This book provides an excellent tool for anyone who is already a leader, or is aspiring to leadership. I highly recommend it.

Jane Hansen Hoyt
President/CEO, Aglow International

I am quite impressed with Dan Hammer's new book, *Servant Leadership*. Dan has gleaned the gold from the writings of many respected leadership trainers and added his own insights from many years of overseeing a local church. This book asks the challenging questions that all leaders need to ask themselves. Dan shares his own struggles to walk out genuine servant leadership himself. I highly recommend this book to leaders and those who would develop a high quality of leadership in their ministries.

Joe McIntyre
Senior Minister
Word of His Grace Church and *The Healing Centre*
Bothell, Washington

Servant
Leadership

Dr. Dan C. Hammer
Foreword by Dr. C. Peter Wagner

Pacific Creek Books
www.pacificcreekbooks.com
An imprint of Paradise Creek Books

Unless otherwise noted, Scripture quotations are from the New Spirit Filled Life Bible, Thomas Nelson Publishing Company, 2002. Used by permission. All rights reserved.

Printed in the United States of America

First Publication: February 2012

ISBN # 978-0-9836652-7-4

Ordering Information
Special discounts are available on quantity purchases. For details, contact Pacific Creek Books at the web address above.

Dedication

I dedicate this workbook to God the Father, Jesus Christ the Son and the Holy Spirit for the love they have poured out on me.

I dedicate this workbook with love to my beautiful wife, Terry, whose servant leadership I have watched for the last 35 years.

Dr. Dan C. Hammer

Contents

Foreword

If my observations are correct, Christian leadership is in a better place today than it was, say, twenty-five years ago. Among other things, I attribute this positive trend to an extraordinary number of leaders who have felt called to multiply their well-honed leadership skills through-out the body of Christ through teaching and writing. One of these is my friend, Dan Hammer, who has forged his leadership know-how through his anchor church in Seattle, Sonrise Christian Center, as well as through his personal apostolic network, Northwest New Wine Network. In fact, among experts who track these kinds of things, there is a consensus that Hammer is broadly considered an apostle to the entire State of Washington. Not many others throughout the U.S. have merited such a prestigious state-wide designation.

With this in mind, it is not surprising that Dan Hammer has crafted one of the most useful workbooks on leader-ship that is available today. As I read the workbook, I was amazed at how much research he had done on contempo-rary literature on leadership as well as on biblical passages that precisely fit every one of the many categories he has outlined. This is not a book to be read from cover to cover in one sitting. It is a workbook to be absorbed a little at a time. In order to aid this process, Dan introduces a shaded box with a number of personal questions every few pages.

If you sit down and determine to answer these questions honestly, either personally or, better yet with a small group, the entire exercise will help you to be a more effective leader no matter where your starting point may be.

I love the adjective, servant leadership. What would be the opposite? I suspect the opposite would be selfish leadership. The choice between the two is a matter of attitude. Why do I lead? Do I lead for the benefit of those who are following me? Or do I lead for my own benefit? This seems like a simple decision—a no brainer. But experience shows that it is not. All too many Christian leaders—especially in the Pentecostal-charismatic camp—have been seekers of personal power. They have developed techniques of manipulating their followers into providing them material and other kinds of privileges that obviously reflect selfishness. Fortunately, as I suggested in the beginning, the trend is away from this kind of selfish leadership into the more healthy servant leadership that Dan Hammer exemplifies and describes in this workbook.

I know Hammer as an apostle. An experienced, tested, recognized apostle. Consequently, his leadership is apostolic leadership. I know this may sound strange to many who are accustomed to traditional American church life. The majority of American church leaders are not apostolic, but rather they are hierarchical. They are employees of someone who oversees them whom they ordinarily did not choose. This is reflected in the leadership structures of whole denominations as well as in local churches where the pastor is an employee of a congregation or of a church board of some kind.

True apostles, on the other hand, do not report to a human agency, but to God. Admittedly, this has dangers but it also has considerable advantages. People follow an apostolic leader, not because someone higher up has appointed him or her, but because they have voluntarily made their decision to follow. Furthermore, there are no legal requirements that compel them to stay. They only need to stay as long as they perceive the leader to be helping them become everything God wants them to be. This arrangement, as you can see, makes servant leadership absolutely essential. Selfish leadership cannot sustain an apostolic following.

I have said all this in order to commend Dan Hammer as a role model for apostolic, servant leadership. Much of what he has learned through the years of implementing this you will find in these pages.

Please read on with excitement, knowing that this dynamic workbook will help bring you to a new level.

C. Peter Wagner,
Vice President and Apostolic Ambassador
Global Spheres, Inc.

Introduction

SERVANT LEADERSHIP

This is a workbook based on my journey for the last ten years – 2000 to 2010. It is a journey to become a better servant leader in the Lord. At Bakke Graduate University I have learned much in relation to servant leadership. The more I have learned, the more I see this will be a lifetime learning experience.

My journey began in 2000 when the Lord spoke to me out of Psalm 78:70-72,

> *"He chose David His servant, And took him from the sheepfolds; From following the ewes that had young He brought him, To shepherd Jacob His people, And Israel His inheritance. So he shepherded them according to the integrity of his heart, And guided them by the skillfulness of his hands."*

God spoke to my heart again and said,

> "The integrity of your heart is not an issue right now, but the skillfulness of your hands is."

I realized I did not have the skills to lead the church I was pastoring, Sonrise Christian Center in Everett, Washington. The Lord led me to Northwest Graduate School, which is now Bakke Graduate University, in Seattle, Washington.

*The more
I have
learned
the more
I see
this will be
a lifetime
learning
experience.*

This helped improve my serving by sharpening my skills and adjusting my attitude.

The overarching theme of the workbook is Servant Leadership. The first chapter will be called Servant Leadership as well, dealing with the basic principles of leaders who serve. My hope is that this workbook will help our staff at Sonrise Christian Center, our ministry in the Fellowship of Christian Assemblies and other local church leaders and ministry leaders to become more effective servant leaders.

What is servant leadership?

The term "servant leadership" is attributed to Robert Greenleaf. Greenleaf was a Quaker involved in the field of organizational management and development.

"The term servant-leadership was coined in a 1970 essay entitled 'The Servant as a Leader,' by Robert K. Greenleaf (1904-1990). Born in Terre Haute, Indiana, Greenleaf spent most of his organizational life in the field of management research, development and education at AT&T. Following a forty-year career at AT&T he enjoyed a second career that lasted twenty-five years. He served as an influential consultant to a number of major institutions, including Ohio University, MIT, Ford Foundation, R.K. Mellon Foundation, the Mead Corporation, the American Foundation of Research, and Lilly Endowment, Inc."[1]

Greenleaf went on to define servant leadership in his own terms.

"The servant-leader is servant first. It begins with the natural feeling that one wants to serve. Then conscious choice brings one to aspire to lead. The best test is: Do those served grow as persons; do they, while being served, become servants? "[2] – Robert Greenleaf

Once a person learns and accepts the role of servant leader, he or she begins to lead other servant leaders.

Once a person learns and accepts the role of servant leader, he or she begins to lead other servant leaders.

In the Bible we see that Jesus Christ is the ultimate example of servant leadership. As a servant leader, He served the Father and the people to whom the Father sent Him to minister.

Mark 10:35-45 says it well:

"Then James and John, the sons of Zebedee, came to Him, saying, 'Teacher, we want You to do for us whatever we ask.' And He said to them, 'What do you want me to do for you?'"

"They said to Him, 'Grant us that we may sit, one on Your right hand and the other on Your left, in Your glory.' But Jesus said to them, 'You do not know what you ask. Are you able to drink the cup that I drink, and be baptized with the baptism that I am baptized with?' They said to Him, 'We are able.' So Jesus said to them, 'You will indeed drink the cup that I drink, and with the baptism I am baptized with you will be baptized; but to sit on My right hand and on My left is not Mine to give, but it is for those for whom it is prepared.' And when the ten heard it, they began to be greatly displeased with James and John. But Jesus called them to Himself and said to them, 'You know that those who are considered rulers over the Gentiles lord it over

them, and their great ones exercise authority of them. Yet it shall not be so among you; but whoever desires to become great among you shall be your servant. And whoever of you desires to be first shall be slave of all. For even the Son of Man did not come to be served but to serve, and to give His life a ransom for many.'"

In this passage Jesus taught His disciples that in order to be great in the Kingdom of God one must serve. Jesus said the Gentiles lord it over people, but that would not be the pattern in His Kingdom. Then He cited His own example as the Son of Man that He came to serve, not to be served and He came to give His life as a ransom for many. We, too, can follow His example of servant leadership, by giving our lives away in service.

Some say the term servant leadership is a paradox and they are right!

> "For some people, the word servant prompts an immediately negative connotation because of the oppression that many workers – particularly women and people of color – have historically endured. For some, it may take a while to accept the positive usage of the word servant. However, those who are willing to dig a little deeper come to understand the inherent spiritual nature of what is intended by the pairing of servant and leader.

...in order to be great in the Kingdom of God one must serve.

The startling paradox of the term servant- leadership serves to prompt new insights."[3]

"Life is full of curious and meaningful paradoxes. Servant-leadership is one such paradox."[4]

In the example of Jesus we see the perfect model of the paradox of servant leadership. He is a servant and He is a leader!

If you want to lead like Jesus, you have to answer three key questions:

1. Am I a leader?_____
   _____
   _____

2. Am I willing to following Jesus as my leadership role model? _____
   _____
   _____

3. How do I lead like Jesus?"_____
   _____
   _____

(Answer these three questions above.)[5]

As I continue my journey to be a servant leader and seek to follow the example of my Lord Jesus, I encourage you to start or continue the journey you have already begun as a servant leader. Ken Blanchard says it well,

"I soon became aware that everything I had ever taught or written on effective leadership during the past thirty-five years, Jesus did to perfection, beyond my ability to portray or describe. I realized that Christians have more in Jesus than just a spiritual leader; we have a practical and effective leadership model for all organizations, for all people, for all situations."[6]

A prayer

"Father, in the name of Jesus, help me to develop servant leadership skills from following Your lead and the attitude of a servant leader from Your heart. Amen."

Chapter One

SERVANT LEADERSHIP

Larry Spears listed ten characteristics of the servant-leader in his book, *Focus on Leadership*.[7]

1. Listening
2. Empathy
3. Healing
4. Awareness
5. Persuasion
6. Conceptualization
7. Foresight
8. Stewardship
9. Commitment to growth of people
10. Building community

He gleaned these from his study on Robert Greenleaf's material. These are great characteristics to see and say to ourselves, "How am I doing in this area?"

I will use an acrostic for the word SERVANT in servant leadership.

How am I doing...?

∫ STANDS FOR SERVANT

How do I serve as a leader?

Matthew 20:26-28:

> *"Yet it shall not be so among you; but whoever desires to become great among you, let him be your servant. And whoever desires to be first among you, let him be your slave – just as the Son of Man did not come to be served, but to serve, and to give His life a ransom for many."*

Serving as a leader in the Kingdom of God is very important. Self-serving or servant leader, which are you?

> "The reality is that we are all self-serving to a degree because we came into this world with self-serving hearts. Is there anything more self-serving than a baby? A baby does not come home from the hospital asking, "Can I help around the house?" The journey of life is to move from a self-serving heart to a serving heart. You finally become an adult when you realize that life is about what you give, rather than what you get."[8]

Leadership in the Kingdom of God is about serving God and ministering to those He gives you. A servant leads by example.

> "A servant leader never asks anyone to do something they wouldn't be willing to do themselves."[9]

" Self-serving or servant leader, which are you? "

"Our example of serving God and others should cause people to want to serve as we do. Jesus came to serve the Father and the people the Father had given Him. Speaking of Jesus, "And what did He come to serve? He came to serve the vision that He had been given by His Father. He came as a teacher, as a leader, as a trainer to prepare people to go out and help other people live according to that vision."[10]

Whom are we serving? How do you see God's vision for them and for us? It is amazing. The more I help and serve others in their vision, the more God helps me with the vision He has given me.

Jesus, a living example

"Now therefore the feast of the Passover, when Jesus knew that His hour had come that He should depart from this world to the Father, having loved His own, who were in the world, He loved them to the end. And supper being ended, the devil having already put it into the heart of Judas Iscariot, Simon's son, to betray Him, Jesus knowing that the Father had given all things into His hands, and that He had come from God and was going to God, rose from supper and laid aside His garments, took a towel and girded Himself.

After that, He poured water into a basin and began to wash the disciples' feet and to wipe them with the towel

What has God been speaking to my heart?

Am I listening?

with which He was girded. Then He came to Simon Peter. And Peter said to Him, 'Lord, are You washing my feet?'

Jesus answered and said to him, 'What I am doing you do not understand now, but you will know after this.'

Peter said to Him, 'You shall never wash my feet!'

Jesus answered him, 'If I do not wash you, you have no part with Me.'

Simon Peter said to Him, 'Lord, not my feet only, but also my hands and my head!'

Jesus said to him, 'He who is bathed needs only to wash his feet, but is completely clean, and you are clean, but not all of you.' For He knew who would betray Him; therefore He said, 'You are not all clean.'

So when He had washed their feet, taken His garments, and sat down again, He said to them, 'Do you know what I have done to you? You call Me Teacher and Lord and you say well, for so I am. If I then, your Lord and Teacher, have washed your feet, you also ought to wash one another's feet. For I have given you an example that you should do as I have done to you.

Most assuredly I say to you, a servant is not greater than his master; nor is he who is sent greater than he *who sent him. If you know these things, blessed are you if you do them.*"[11]

What an amazing passage. It says that the Father had given all things into His hands. So what did He do with all that power and authority? Probably something we would not have done without His example … wash the disciples' feet.

Peter said in verse 8,

"You shall never wash my feet!"

How wrong Peter was with that statement. Jesus told Peter in verse 8,

"If I do not wash you, you have no part with Me."

"I have had my feet washed by people who love me, and I have washed the feet of people I love in order to serve them. But how else can we wash people's feet and be obedient to Jesus? What did Jesus become obedient to? The part we left out says that He died a selfless, obedient death – and the worst kind of death at that: a crucifixion. Jesus, the best example of a servant leader, paid a price in order to express God's love to others. On the character ladder, we must also pay a price. What price? Within the boundaries of loving others, the payment will be different for each of us."[12]

We can serve God and others by listening to them and being obedient to whatever God tells us to do.

Listening as a servant leader

As a servant leader we must first listen to God and serve Him. Paul showed this principle in II Corinthians 8:5,

"And not only as we had hoped, but they first gave themselves to the Lord, and then to us by the will of God."

We first serve and listen to God and then we listen and serve others. It is so important as a servant leader.

"Leaders have traditionally been valued for their communication and decision-making skills. These are also important skills for the servant-leader, but they need to be reinforced by a deep commitment to listening intently to others. The servant-leader seeks to identify the will of a group and to help clarify that will. He or she seeks to listen receptively to what is being said (and not said!)"[13]

What has God been speaking to my heart?

Am I listening? Reflect on it.

What are the people I see saying or not saying?

What am I hearing? Reflect on it!

> *What has God been speaking to my heart? Am I listening?*

Questions

1. Whom are you serving? _____

    _____

    _____

    _____

    _____

2. How are you serving God? _____

    _____

    _____

    _____

    _____

3. Look back at the list of ten characteristics of a servant leader. Which are you doing well? _____

    _____

    _____

    _____

    _____

4. Which need growth?_____

    _____

    _____

    _____

    _____

5. What steps will you take to change? _____

    _____

    _____

    _____

    _____

...part of
our
service
as a
servant
leader is
to help
others
become
more
effective
in ministry.

$\mathcal{E}$ STANDS FOR EQUIPPING

A servant leader is called to equip others to do the work of the ministry, so part of our service as a servant leader is to help others become more effective in ministry.

"And He Himself gave some to be apostles, some prophets, some evangelists, and some pastors and teachers, for the equipping of the saints, for the work of ministry, for the edifying of the body of Christ, till we all come to the unity of the faith and of the knowledge of the Son of God, to a perfect man, to the measure of the stature of the fullness of Christ; that we should no longer be children, tossed to and fro and carried about with every wind of doctrine, by the trickery of men, in the cunning craftiness of deceitful plotting, but, speaking the truth in love, may grow up in all things into Him who is the head – Christ – from whom the whole body, joined and knit together by what every joint supplies, according to the effective working by which every part does its share, causes growth of the body of the edifying of itself in love."[14]

Equipping the saints

"There are gifted men given to the church for the perfecting of the saints. The word 'perfecting' is Katartizo, to equip for service. These gifted men are to specialize in equipping the saints for the 'work of the ministry,' that is, for ministering work, in short,

Christian service."[15] These gifts are used to build up
the body of Christ to bring it to maturity. "Kat-or-
tis-moss is the Greek word for equipping. It means
"A making fit, preparing, training, perfecting, making
fully qualified for service."[16]

Our privilege as a servant leader is to help others be made
fit, prepared, trained and perfected as a people to do the
work God has given them to do. We are building people
up to do what God wants them to do and to become what
God wants them to become. The idea of "perfecting the
saints" is to bring a person to full maturity in Christ. It
is important to know what God has called a person to do
to be able to equip them. The more as leaders we know
people's hearts and dreams, the easier it is to help them.
Every saint is called to do the work of the ministry. "Give
them what you got" and refer them to someone else for
what you do not have.

Empowering people

Jesus was constantly empowering people.

> "In the use of His time and efforts on earth, Jesus
> modeled sacrificial passion for ensuring that His fol-
> lowers were equipped to carry on the movement."[17]

He was constantly training, modeling and teaching people
how to live life and do the work of the ministry.

Paul the Apostle was relentlessly equipping people to be disciples of Jesus Christ. In Ephesians 4 he talked about equipping people to do the work of the ministry.

In II Timothy 2:2, it says,

> *"And the things that you have heard from me among many witnesses, commit these to faithful men who will be able to teach others also."*

Paul poured into faithful men just as Jesus did to empower them for ministry. We pour into people and release them to pour into others.

...empower others by pouring into them what God has poured into you!

GOD poured into

PAUL, who poured into

TIMOTHY, who poured into

OTHERS

II Timothy 2:2

You empower others by
pouring into them what
God has poured into you!

Questions

1. Are you equipping and pouring into others?_____

   _____

   _____

   _____

   _____

2. What do they need? _____

   _____

   _____

   _____

   _____

$\mathcal{R}$ IS FOR RELATIONSHIP

Relationship is so important to being a servant leader. Having a great relationship with God and others is vital to dynamic servant leadership. The more we get to know someone in a relationship, the easier it is to serve them.

"Let love be without hypocrisy. Abhor what is evil. Cling to what is good. Be kindly affectionate to one another with brotherly love, in honor giving preference to one another; not lagging in diligence, fervent in spirit, serving the Lord; rejoicing in hope, patient in tribulations, continuing steadfastly in prayer; distributing to the needs of the saints, given to hospitality.

Bless those who persecute you; bless and do not curse. Rejoice with those who rejoice, and weep with those who weep. Be of the same mind toward one another. Do not set your mind on high things, but associate with the humble. Do not be wise in your own opinion. Repay to no one evil for evil. Have regard for good things in the sight of all men. If it is possible, as much as depends on you, live peaceably with all men.

Beloved, do not avenge yourselves but rather give place to wrath; for it is written, "vengeance is Mine, I will repay," says the Lord. Therefore, "If your enemy hungers,

The more we get to know someone in a relationship, the easier it is to serve them.

feed him; If he thirsts, give him drink; For in so doing you will heap coals of fire on his head."

Do not be overcome by evil, but overcome evil with good."[18]

This passage is about relationship. It gives some vital keys to building relationships as a servant leader.

1. Let love be without hypocrisy
2. Abhor what is evil – cling to the good
3. Be kindly affectionate to one another
4. In honor prefer one another
5. Be diligent
6. Be fervent in spirit
7. Serve the Lord
8. Rejoice in hope – be patient – continue in prayer
9. Distribute to the needs of others – be hospitable
10. Associate with the humble
11. Do not be wise in your own opinion
12. Do not repay evil for evil
13. Live at peace with people
14. Overcome evil with good.

The things in this passage point directly or indirectly to relationships. Relationships can involve love, encouragement, advice, correction, care, challenge and hope.

"In today's world, leaders must be able to help people in the organization realize their human potential. They must also be able to lead during a time of instability, uncertainty and continuous change. To do so, leaders must be emotionally flexible, paradoxical, non-defensive, empathetic and values- driven. In short, leaders must model authenticity."[19]

Paul gave some practical examples of helping people perfect their human potential by loving, seeing, knowing, etc.

Questions

1. In this passage, which of these are your strengths? _____

    _____

    _____

    _____

    _____

    _____

2. In this passage, which of these need work?____

    _____

    _____

    _____

    _____

    _____

V IS FOR VULNERABILITY

"Confess your trespasses to one another, and pray for one another, that you may be healed. The effective fervent prayer of a righteous man avails much."[20]

To be a servant leader requires vulnerability. Vulnerability is the ability to be open to attack or intrusion. It means to let down your guard.

In James 5:16, it talks about confessing our trespasses to one another and praying for one another. There is a deep level of relationship that takes place when we open up our hearts to each other.

Relational transparency is important in being a servant leader. "It is not enough to be self-aware, congruent in values and actions, and objective in one's interpretations; an authentic leader must also be willing to communicate this information in an open and honest manner with others through self-disclosure."[21]

It is easier for others to be open to you if you are open and vulnerable to them. One way to open people's hearts is to affirm them with words and actions. Honoring people this way will help build an incredible bond.

To be a servant leader requires vulnerability.

"The principle of honor states that: accurately ac-knowledging who people are will position us to give them what they desire and to receive the gift of who they are in our lives."[22]

Affirming people and knowing them creates an opening for access to them and they to you. Paul had this experi-ence with the Corinthians in II Corinthians 6:11-13,

"O Corinthians! We have spoken openly to you, our heart is wide open. You are not restricted by us, but you are restricted by your own affections. Now in return for the same (I speak as to children), you also be open."

Paul and his companions had opened their hearts wide to the Corinthians but the Corinthians were not open to Paul. He was now encouraging the Corinthians to change. Openness is a vital part of being a servant leader.

A personal illustration

I remember a time in a staff meeting when I was telling my staff I was too busy and did not have enough time for them. One of the staff was bothered and said I was not listening to them. So at a meeting another time, my wife and I poured out our hearts and shared how we felt we were carrying the whole load of the church and how hard it was (my wife and I were both crying). The one who was bothered before said, "Yes! Yes! This is what we want –

this is like the day before Christmas." Her heart was crying for vulnerability, transparency and openness. SOMETHING NEW STARTED IN THE CHURCH THAT DAY. SOMETHING NEW TO ME! The staff opened up their hearts that day because my wife and I had opened our hearts and made ourselves vulnerable.

Questions

1. What opens up your heart?_____

   _____

   _____

2. What keeps you from being vulnerable?_____

   _____

   _____

   _____

3. To whom can I confess and pray with for my needs? _____

   _____

   _____

4. As a servant leader, what decision can you make to open up your heart?_____

   _____

   _____

Lord, in Jesus' name help me open my heart to You and others You have brought into my life. Amen.

The staff opened up their hearts that day because my wife and I had opened our hearts and made ourselves vulnerable.

𝒶 IS FOR ASSIST

Being a servant leader is assisting people to become all God wants them to be. To assist someone means to help them. Today there are many assisted-care living facilities. These facilities help people who cannot live independently. In the Church, we are to assist each other to become the people God wants us to be – we are dependent upon God and others for this to happen.

> *"Let us hold fast the confession of our hope without wavering, for He who promised is faithful. And let us consider one another in order to stir up love and good works, not forsaking the assembling of ourselves together, as is the manner of some, but exhorting one another, and so much the more as you see the day approaching."*[23]

We can assist each other by stirring up love and good works and melding together. We should encourage one another when we gather together, especially as we see the end approaching.

One of the best questions we can ask each other as we work for the Lord is, "How can I help you? How can I assist people I am working with in the church and in God's Kingdom to become leaders?"

"Authentic leadership was first defined by Luthans and Avolio (2003) as a process described as being a style which results in both greater self-awareness and self-regulated positive behaviors on the part of leaders and associates, fostering positive self-development. The authentic leader is confident, hopeful, optimistic, resilient, transparent, moral/ethical, future-oriented, and gives priority to developing associates to be leaders."[24]

How can I help you become the leader God wants you to be? Self-awareness is one of the major keys needed to develop as a servant leader.

Questions

1. Who is assisting you? _____
   _____
   _____
   _____

2. How is your self-awareness developing? _____
   _____
   _____

   Or isn't it? _____
   _____
   _____

3. How can I help you? _____
   _____
   _____
   _____

How can I help you become the leader God wants you to be?

/V IS FOR NURTURE

Nurture is helping someone in their growth and development. As a servant leader, we nurture people in their character development.

> *"…but speaking the truth in love, may grow up in all things into Him who is the head – Christ – for whom the whole body, joined and knit together by what every joint supplies, according to the effective working by which every part does its share, causes growth of the body for the edifying of itself in love."*[25]

In the context of this passage, it is talking about the five-fold ministry of Jesus that He gave: apostles, prophets, evangelists, pastors and teachers to equip the saints (every believer). Equip the saints so that the Body of Christ may grow up and be edified in love and every member can do their part.

Two important parts of nurture

There are two important things to keep in mind when developing as a servant leader and developing other servant leaders. One is character development, and the other is a right attitude. God wants to produce godly character in His servant leaders. "Integrity is the heart of character."[26]

God allows character to be tested.

> "But also for this very reason, giving all diligence,
> add to your faith virtue, to virtue knowledge, to
> knowledge self-control, to self-control perseverance,
> to perseverance godliness, to godliness brotherly
> kindness, and to brotherly kindness love. For if
> these things are yours and abound, you will be nei-
> ther barren nor unfruitful in the knowledge of our
> Lord Jesus Christ."[27]

God is forming His character in us. As we pass the tests,
He can enlarge our ministry and influence. We mature
and grow in character one obedience at a time!

God wants a servant leader's attitude to be right. You
are personally responsible for your attitude. Attitude is a
choice. A servant leader should have an attitude of humility, thankfulness, generosity, loving, caring, enthusiasm
and serving, to name just a few.

You are personally responsible for your attitude. Attitude is a choice.

> *Servant leaders are teachers by example and word.*

Questions

1. How is your attitude? _____
    _____
    _____
    _____
    _____

2. Do you need an attitude adjustment? _____
    _____
    _____
    _____
    _____

3. Where is God working on your character? ____
    _____
    _____
    _____
    _____

4. Whom are you nurturing? _____
    _____
    _____
    _____
    _____

5. Who is nurturing you? _____
    _____
    _____
    _____
    _____

$\mathcal{T}$ IS FOR TEACHING

In Ephesians 4:11-16 we see teachers are called to equip the saints and bring them to a place of maturity in Christ. Servant leaders are teachers by example and word. Luke wrote,

> *"The former account I made, O Theophilus, of all that Jesus began both to do and teach, until the day in which He was taken up, after He through the Holy Spirit had given commandments to the apostles whom He had chosen, to whom He also presented Himself alive after His suffering by many infallible proofs, being seen by them during forty days and speaking of the things pertaining to the Kingdom of God."[28]*

We, too, as servant leaders need to teach what pertains to the Kingdom of God. Jesus and the apostles taught with the purpose of putting their teaching into action.

New skills are needed

Teach servant leaders new skills of leadership. As we have entered the twenty-first century, it is obvious many new skills are needed for leaders. Some of the most important leadership skills are found in *Cases in Leadership*:

> "Skills suggest what leaders can achieve, whereas traits suggest who they are based on their intrinsic characteristics."[29]

"Katz's (1974) seminal article on the skills approach to leadership suggested that leadership (i.e., effective administration) is based on three skills: technical, human, and conceptual."[30]

Technical skills are needed to be competent on how things work. Human skills are needed to work with people. Conceptual skills are needed to think through ideas for the future and improve the ability to articulate them and/or write them down on paper.

How would you handle someone who is not being effective in their particular ministry?

Questions

1. What skills do you need to develop in the technical area?_____

   _____

2. What human skills do you need to develop? _

   _____

   _____

3. What skills do you need to develop conceptual thinking? _____

   _____

   _____

   _____

New models are needed

One new model may be to develop problem-solving questions to discuss and think about together with your leadership team, such as: How would you handle someone who is not being effective in their particular ministry?

You might discover new methods and model ways to address these types of situations as you develop leaders in your church or ministry.

Conclusion

Servant leaders are needed! You can be developed and develop other servant leaders. I believe God wants us to be leaders of leaders, not leaders of followers. You can be creative in your teaching. Remember…

Serve

Equip

Relationships

Vulnerability

Assist

Nurture

Teach

The overarching principle of this workbook is servant leadership. Servant leadership is modeled by Jesus Christ. How is your service to God and to others? How could you improve your service?

Chapter Two

SUPERNATURAL LEADERSHIP

In the twenty-first century there has been an upswing of people looking at the supernatural. God's journey for my life has been with the Pentecostal Evangelical church through thirty-five years of following Him. My journey began on August 11, 1975, when in the middle of a nervous breakdown I gave my life to Jesus Christ as I read *The Cross and the Switchblade*[31]. I was saved and delivered from demonic bondage. My ministry has involved signs and wonders and seeing the Holy Spirit make Jesus Christ and the Father real to people. To be a servant leader in the twenty-first century we must know the supernatural power of God.

Paul says it well in I Corinthians 2:1-5:

> *"And I, brethren, when I came to you, did not come with excellence of speech or of wisdom declaring to you the testimony of God. For I determined not to know anything among you except Jesus Christ and Him crucified. I was with you in weakness, in fear and in much trembling. And my speech and my preaching were not with persuasive words of human wisdom, but in demonstration of the Spirit of power, that your faith should not be in the wisdom of men but in the power of God."*

Our faith should be in the demonstration of the Spirit and of power. Paul wanted the faith of the Corinthians not to be in the wisdom of men, but he wanted it to be in the power of God. We need God's supernatural power to be servant leaders in the twenty-first century just as they did in Paul's day in Corinth.

We need to not only be natural, but SUPERnatural. I have identified an acrostic, S-U-P-E-R, to look at supernatural leadership or servant leader.

> *We need to not only be natural, but SUPER natural!*

$\mathcal{S}$ STANDS FOR SEEKING LEADERSHIP

To be involved with supernatural leadership, it is important to seek the Lord with the purpose toward intimate relationship with Him.

> "Supernatural means existing outside the forces of nature, miraculous or divine, of ghosts, demons, etc."[32]

The supernatural leadership I will discuss is the miraculous power of God.

Seek to be intimate

The purpose of seeking God is to be intimate with Him. In Daniel 11:32 it says,

> *"Those who do wickedly against the covenant he shall corrupt with flattery; but the people who know their God shall be strong, and carry out great exploits."*

To walk in supernatural leadership it is vital to be intimate with God. Isaiah 50:4 talks about the intimacy Jesus had with the Father.

In Isaiah 50:4-7 it reads,

"The Lord God has given Me the tongue of the learned, that I should know how to speak a word in season to him who is weary. He awakens Me morning by morning. He awakens My ear to hear as the learned. The Lord God has opened My ear; and I was not rebellious, nor did I turn away. I gave My back to those who struck Me, and My cheeks to those who plucked out the beard; I did not hide My face from shame and spitting. For the Lord God will help Me; therefore I will not be disgraced; therefore I have set My face like a flint, and I know that I will not be ashamed."

The Father awakened Jesus' ear morning by morning so Jesus could speak with the tongue of the learned; because He had the ear of the learned He listened to what the Father said, then did it. He was not rebellious and did not turn out of the way the Father led Him. He was then able to speak a word of refreshing to those who were weary.

To walk in supernatural leadership it is vital to be intimate with God.

In John 5:19-20 it states,

> "Then Jesus answered and said to them, 'Most assuredly, I say to you, the Son can do nothing of Himself, but what He sees the Father do; for whatever He does, the Son also does in like manner. For the Father loves the Son, and shows Him all things that He Himself does, and He will show Him greater works than these, that you may marvel.'"

The early Church

In Acts the apostles and church continued to hear God's supernatural voice.

Acts 13:1, 2,

> "Now in the church that was at Antioch there were certain prophets and teachers: Barnabas, Simeon who was called Niger, Lucius of Cyrene, Manaen who had been brought up with Herod the tetrarch, and Saul. As they ministered to the Lord and fasted, the Holy Spirit said, 'Now separate to Me Barnabas and Saul for the work to which I have called them.'"

As we seek the Lord and worship Him, He speaks to our hearts. He told them to separate Saul and Barnabas for the work of missions He had given to them.

Seeking brings wisdom and revelation

One of Paul's prayers in Ephesians was that God would grant the spirit of wisdom and revelation to them.

Ephesians 1:15-23 says,

"Therefore I also, after I heard of your faith in the Lord Jesus and your love for all the saints, do not cease to give thanks for you, making mention of you in my prayers: that the God of our Lord Jesus Christ, the Father of glory may give to you the spirit of wisdom and revelation in the knowledge of Him, the eyes of your understanding being enlightened; that you may know what is the hope of His calling, what are the riches of the glory of His inheritance in the saints, and what is the exceeding greatness of His power toward us who believe, according to the working of His mighty power which He worked in Christ when He raised Him from the dead and seated Him at His right hand in the heavenly places, far above all principality and power and might and dominion and every name that is named, not only in the age but also in that which is to come. And He put all things under His feet and gave Him to be head over all things to the church, which is His body, the fullness of Him who fills all in all."

God wants to reveal things to us and give us wisdom from heaven.

God wants to reveal things to us and give us wisdom from heaven.

In 1 Corinthians 2:9, 10, it says,

> *"But it is written: 'Eye has not seen, nor ear heard, nor have entered into the heart of man the things which God has prepared for those who love Him.' But God has revealed them to us through His Spirit. For the Spirit searches all things, yes, the deep things of God."*

God reveals things to our eyes and ears that enter our heart by the Holy Spirit, who indwells us. This causes us to walk in supernatural leadership.

Questions

1. How are you intimate with the Lord? _____
   _____
   _____

2. How are you seeking Him? _____
   _____
   _____

3. Do you need the spirit of wisdom and revelation regarding something specific?_____
   _____
   _____

Seek Him!

U STANDS FOR UNUSUAL SIGNS

Signs, wonders and miracles

In Acts 19:11, 12 says,

> *"Now God worked unusual miracles by the hands*
> *of Paul, so that even handkerchiefs or aprons were*
> *brought from his body to the sick, and the diseases left*
> *them and the evil spirits went out of them."*

God is a supernatural God who works miracles in people's lives. If there are unusual miracles, there must be usual miracles. I believe the greatest miracle is Jesus Christ becoming the Lord and Savior of our life and forgiving our sins.

> "I love the way Luke uses the phrase unusual miracles. The immediate implication is that if some miracles are unusual then other miracles must be usual or ordinary. Compared to no miracles at all, any miracle might be regarded as unusual. But in places where the Holy Spirit is moving in a revival atmosphere and where miracles are not uncommon, we do find ourselves even today distinguishing unusual miracles from the ordinary ones."[33]

All throughout the Bible with Moses, Daniel, Hannah, Ezekiel, Luke, Paul, Mary and Joseph, Peter and others, God did miracles!

I have had the privilege to see God work many signs, wonders and miracles during the last thirty-five years of my ministry. One took place in our church when a member of our congregation named Irma Sullivan was healed by the Lord! She had a rotted kidney and bladder, heart problems and lupus. Three years later, she is still healed. God is awesome! He works supernaturally. I thank God for doctors and all the medical breakthroughs that help people, but I am so thankful for the power in the Name of Jesus Christ of Nazareth. This must have been just as it happened in Acts 3 when the man with deformed ankles was healed.

Mark 16:19, 20 says,

> *"So then, after the Lord had spoken to them, He was received up into heaven, and sat down at the right hand of God. And they went out and preached everywhere, the Lord working with them and confirming the word through the accompanying signs. Amen."*

God will work with us as we preach His Word. Signs, wonders and miracles follow His Word to confirm it. The signs should always point people to Jesus Christ, not to us.

Signs, wonders and miracles today

Two ministries/leaders have had a tremendous impact on my life. One is John Wimber and the Vineyard Fellowship

...signs should always point people to Jesus Christ, not to us.

in Anaheim, California, and the other is Bill Johnson and Bethel Church in Redding, California.

John Wimber taught me how to work with God. He taught me to recognize when God is doing something I should *join* Him and work alongside Him. I learned much through John Wimber's ministry before he died.

God has used unusual signs, wonders and miracles to draw people to Himself. Not everyone who sees these things are drawn to Him, but many have been moved to Him this way.

> "If you've heard of Bethel Church in Redding, California, chances are that you've heard testimonies of the supernatural happenings that take place there on a regular basis, particularly instances of healing. What you may not have heard is that these supernatural events are directly related to the supernatural culture that the community of saints at Bethel has been developing for a decade. The heart of this culture is the conviction that Jesus modeled the Christian life for us. Jesus explained that all the supernatural things that happened through Him flowed directly from His intimate connection with His Father, and that same connection was what He came to give us through His death and resurrection."[34]

At Bethel Church, Bill Johnson and his team have seen a supernatural culture emerging, affecting many people's lives.

At this time, the church is ripe for apostolic leaders to arise. I believe the apostolic gift in Ephesians 4:11-16 and I Corinthians 12:29 is more about function than title. Reggie McNeal tells about it in *Back to the Future: Apostolic Churches*:

> "Leadership for a new apostolic era has a distinctive character to it. It is captured by and reflects the heart of God. Apostolic leadership seeks to partner with God in his redemptive mission in the world. Leaders of this ilk commit themselves to an agenda bent on transforming the world. This revolution begins with a different way of doing church."[35]

At this time, the church is ripe for apostolic leaders to arise.

In his chapter on *"Back to the Future: Apostolic Churches,"* he stresses four shifts that need to be made in our paradigms. These shifts are quoted below:

Future paradigm shifts

1. Top-down to Flat Line – the empowering of the saints;

2. From Inside to Inside-Out – Christians sent into the world

3. From Outside to Outside-in – meets people where they are – outside;

4. From the Edge to the Center – Kingdom back in the center of society.[36]

Along with unusual signs, wonders and miracles, apostolic order is needed such as Reggie McNeal suggests. In I Corinthians 12:28 it says God set first in the church apostles. Part of the apostolic church's ministry was to see signs and wonders.

II Corinthians 12:12 says,

> *"Truly the signs of an apostle were accomplished among you with all perseverance, in signs and wonders and mighty deeds."*

One of the apostolic church's characteristics is for signs, wonders and miracles to occur.

Questions

1. Do you believe signs, wonders and miracles are for today? _____

   _____

2. Have you been used to see God's power manifested?_____

   _____

   _____

   _____

   _____

   _____

   _____

𝒫 STANDS FOR POWER

Paul makes it very clear in I Corinthians 4:20,

"For the kingdom of God is not in word but in power."

God wants His supernatural power to transform people. In Acts 1:8, it says,

"But you shall receive power when the Holy Spirit has come upon you; and you shall be witnesses to Me in Jerusalem, and in all Judea and Samaria, and to the end of the earth."

We receive the power of the Holy Spirit to be witnesses unto Jesus! People need the power of God to work in them to see their lives changed.

In Ephesians 3:20, Paul told the church at Ephesus,

"Now to Him who is able to do exceedingly abundantly above all that we ask or think, according to the power that works in us..."

We must let His power work in us to see those things that He can do exceedingly abundantly above our asking and thinking abilities! God is a supernatural God who wants supernatural leadership!

God wants His supernatural power to transform people.

His power, His person and His presence

Along with His power, His person and His presence are needed as well. We need to uplift the person of Jesus Christ as Philippians 2:9 says,

> "*Therefore God also has highly exalted Him and given Him the name which is above every name.*"

As we see His power, we need to declare His person – who He is! Along with His power and His person, we need to declare His presence. In Psalm 16:11, David said,

> "*You will show me the path of life; In Your presence is fullness of joy; at Your right hand are pleasures forevermore.*"

His presence is important to supernatural ministry leadership. All three of these are vital to keep supernatural leadership in balance.

Questions

1. Are you walking and moving in the power of the Holy Spirit? _____

2. Do you know His presence and His person?

   _____

3. Are you filled with His Holy Spirit? _____

4. Are you a witness of Him? How? _____

   _____

Supernatural leaders should always have a desire to evangelize by making disciples of all nations.

$\mathcal{E}$ STANDS FOR EVANGELISM

Evangelism with the goal of making disciples

Supernatural leaders should always have a desire to evangelize by making disciples of all nations. Mark 16:15-18,

"And He said to them, 'Go into all the world and preach the gospel to every creature. He who believes and is baptized will be saved; but he who does not believe will be condemned. And these signs will follow those who believe: In My name they will cast out demons; they will speak with new tongues; they will take up serpents, and if they drink anything deadly, it will by no means hurt them; they will lay hands on the sick, and they will recover.'"

This is power evangelism. In the Book of Acts, we see many power encounters that bring people to Jesus…

- Acts 2 – On the day of Pentecost
- Acts 3 – The lame man healed at the Beautiful Gate
- Acts 4 – With great power the apostles gave witness to the resurrection
- Acts 5 – Ananias and Sapphira struck dead
- Acts 6 – Disciples are multiplying
- Acts 7 – The story of Stephen and his vision alerts Saul

- Acts 8 – Philip's ministry in Samaria
- Acts 9 – Saul's conversion

…and on and on in the Book of Acts we have examples of God's power through evangelism bringing people into the Kingdom. All through the New Testament from Jesus with the woman at the well (John 4), Paul with the woman who had a spirit of divination in Acts 16, Jesus speaking to the wind and sea in Mark 4 and the like, are full of power evangelism.

Evangelism through serving

God gave the disciples authority to call on His power and to expect it to show up and Him as well.

Matthew 10:1-15 states,

"And when He had called His twelve disciples to Him, He gave them power over unclean spirits, to cast them out, and to heal all kinds of sickness and all kinds of disease.

Now the names of the twelve apostles are these: first, Simon, who is called Peter, and Andrew his brother; James the son of Zebedee, and John his brother; Philip and Bartholomew; Thomas and Matthew the tax collector; James the son of Alphaeus, and Lebbaeus, whose surname was Thaddaeus; Simon the Canaanite and Judas Iscariot, who also betrayed Him. These twelve

Jesus sent out and commanded them, saying, 'Do not go into the way of the Gentiles, and do not enter a city of the Samaritans. But go rather to the lost sheep of the house of Israel. And as you go, preach, saying, 'The kingdom of heaven is at hand.''

"Heal the sick, cleanse the lepers, raise the dead, cast out demons. Freely you have received, freely give. Provide neither gold nor silver nor copper in your money belts, nor bag for your journey, nor two tunics, nor sandals, nor staffs, for a worker is worthy of his food. Now whatever city or town you enter inquire who in it is worthy, and stay there till you go out. And when you go into a household, greet it. If the household is worthy, let your peace come upon it. But if it is not worthy, let your peace return to you. And whoever will not receive you nor hear your words, when you depart from that house or city, shake off the dust from your feet."

"Assuredly, I say to you, it will be more tolerable for the land of Sodom and Gomorrah in the day of judgment than for that city!"

> *He has given us authority to evangelize in power with the goal to make disciples.*

He has given us authority to evangelize in power with the goal to make disciples. Disciples are disciplined followers of Jesus who know Him as Lord and serve Him daily. Remember in John 13 when all things were given into Jesus' hands by the Father? He used this power to wash his disciples' feet. We too have been given power to serve. In evangelism we serve by providing the gospel of the Kingdom. C. Peter Wagner, in his commentary of Acts, lists 15 signs of the Kingdom from Isaiah 61, Luke 7:23, and Mark 16:15-18 quoted here:

1. Preaching the gospel to the poor
2. Healing the brokenhearted
3. Preaching deliverance to the captives
4. Restoring sight to the blind
5. Liberating the oppressed
6. Instituting the acceptable year of the Lord
7. Healing the sick
8. Casting out evil spirits
9. Miraculously having people walk
10. Cleansing lepers
11. Restoring hearing to the deaf
12. Raising the dead
13. Speaking in new tongues
14. Safety when picking up serpents
15. Immunity to poison

R STANDS FOR RELEASING THE SAINTS

In Ephesians 4:11-16 it states that apostles, prophets, evangelists, pastors, and teachers are to equip the saints to do the work of the ministry and to bring each believer to a place of maturity.

In Proverbs 18:16 it states,

"A man's gift makes room for him, And brings him before great men."

Your gifts can make a place for you to minister.

Recognize, raise up and release!

Michael Adams summarizes this concept well.

"I believe that is the one and only true mission of those that consider themselves '5-fold ministers.' Why? To equip means to train – to supply with the tools, provisions and qualities necessary for performance. Proverbs 22:6 says, 'Train up a child in the way he should go, even when he is old he will not depart from it.' You cannot effectively equip someone to succeed without taking the time to do these three process steps:

Effective equipping steps

1. <u>Recognize</u> their existing gifts, skills, yearnings and limitations.

2. <u>Raise them up</u> by helping them to develop and effectively use their strengths and overcome their weaknesses, and then

3. <u>Release</u> them into their own Great Commission assignment as revealed by God."[37]

The more you get to know people the easier it is to release them. Work to <u>recognize</u>, <u>raise</u> up and then <u>release</u> them.

The more you get to know people the easier it is to release them.

A practical way to help release

Meeting regularly with my staff has helped us get to know each other so I can help release them into their assignment.

> "If you, as a servant in authority, want to be an effective shepherd to those whom God has entrusted to you to recognize, raise up and release, then use of both a job description and performance management review will help you keep in close touch with those whom you serve and those who serve with you."[38]

When dealing with pastors and staff, I find many do not have a clear job description, regular review or a vision and goals for the church/ministry they serve! This makes ministry very difficult.

Questions

1. Have you been recognized, raised up and released? _____

   _____

2. Are you doing the same for others?_____

   _____

   _____

3. Do you have a clear job description, goals and a regular review? _____

   _____

Chapter Three

STRATEGIC LEADERSHIP

One aspect of being a servant leader is to be involved in Strategic Leadership. Strategies are needed to help a church ministry move forward in its calling.

> "Ireland and Hitt (1999) define strategic leadership as the ability to participate, envision, maintain flexibility, think strategically, and work with others to initiate changes that will locate a viable future for the agencies. p. 43"[39]

God can give us the strategy we need for different expectations in life and ministry. I will use the acrostic S-T-R-A-T-E-G-Y to look at different aspects of strategic leadership principles.

S STANDS FOR STRATEGIC THINKING

Sometimes I think we do strategic planning before we do strategic thinking. It is important to realize that strategic leadership needs to begin with what God is saying. Let's think with God and each other before we plan.

"Sometimes I think we do strategic planning before we do strategic thinking."

Ephesians 5:15-17 says,

"See then that you walk circumspectly, not as fools but
as wise, redeeming the time, because the days are evil.
Therefore do not be unwise, but understand what the
will of the Lord is."

It is important to "buy" the opportunities God gives us
so we can use them for maximum advantage. Strategic
thinking helps define, "What will the end look like?" Then
we can plot strategic steps with God's help and the help of
others to see how to meet each desired goal.

This type of strategic thinking will bring focus and help
us design the necessary steps to accomplish the task. This
strategic, visionary thinking makes us all of like mind.
Ken Blanchard and Phil Hodges put it well.

"Our point of view is that vision and implement-ation
are two sides of the same coin – each equally impor-
tant. To maximize results for everyone concerned,
we must lead by setting course and direction, and
then we 'flip the coin.'"[40]

Paul had a vision from God given him on the road to
Damascus. In Acts 26:19 he said,

"Therefore, King Agrippa, I was not disobedient to the
heavenly vision."

*It is
important
to "buy"
the
opportunities
God
gives us
so we can
use them for
maximum
advantage.*

While implementing the vision God gave him, Paul empowered and supported others. How are you empowering and supporting others as you implement your corporate vision?

T STANDS FOR THEOLOGICALLY SOUND

In our strategic leadership as servant leaders, it is important to build on the foundation of Jesus Christ and the Word of God. Isaiah 46:10 says,

> *"Declaring the end from the beginning, and from ancient times things that are not yet done, saying, 'My counsel shall stand, and I will do all My pleasure.'"*

And in Luke 6:46-69 Jesus said,

> *"But why do you call me 'Lord, Lord,' and not do the things which I say? Whoever comes to Me, and hears My sayings and does them, I will show you whom he is like; He is like a man building a house, who dug deep and laid the foundation on the rock. And when the flood arose, the stream beat vehemently against that house, and could not shake it, for it was founded on the rock. But he who heard and did nothing is like a man who built a house on the earth without a foundation, against which the stream beat vehemently; and immediately it fell. And the ruin of the house was great."*

We need to hear Jesus' sayings and do them. In II Timothy 4:1-5 Paul instructs Timothy about theological and doctrinal soundness,

> *"I charge you therefore before God and the Lord Jesus Christ, who will judge the living and the dead at His appearing and His kingdom; preach the word! Be ready in season and out of season. Convince, rebuke, exhort, with all long-suffering and teaching. For the time will come when they will not endure sound doctrine, but according to their own desires, because they have itching ears, they will heap up for themselves teachers; and they will turn their ears away from the truth, and be turned aside to fables. But you be watchful in all things, endure afflictions, do the work of an evangelist, fulfill your ministry."*

It helps people to know the foundation of God's Word in order to build their strategies upon it. We need to hear what God says and do it. It is clear that we need to love and build *people* up, as well as strategies, based on God's Word.

R STANDS FOR RESOURCES

Everyone is in need of resources. It is helpful to know what resources are available to you in ministry. From my perspective there are three valuable resources we all need.

> *It is clear that we need to love and build people up, as well as strategies...*

Resource number one

The first and most important resource is God. What is God saying and what is God doing?

In John 5:19, 20 Jesus said,

> *"Most assuredly I say to you, the Son can do nothing of Himself, but what He sees the Father do for whatever He does, the Son also does in like manner. For the Father loves the Son, and shows Him all things that He Himself does; and He will show Him greater works than these, that you may marvel."*

Jesus only did what He saw the Father doing. We need to do what the Father and the Son are doing and say what they are saying. This comes out of spending time with God in intimacy and being in the Word of God.

You can look to God as your greatest resource. In Matthew 6:33, Jesus said,

> *"But seek first the kingdom of God and His righteousness, and all these things shall be added to you."*

In its context, Jesus was telling us not to worry, God will help you!

Resource number two

The second greatest resource is people. All people have unique gifts and talents. I Corinthians 12-14 tells about the different gifts in the Body of Christ: apostles, prophets, tongues, helps, administration, healings, word of knowledge, word of wisdom and so on. People who know, develop and use their gifts as God directs are key to advancing the Kingdom of God on earth.

Many times I notice the very people I need are right in front of me, if I will look. With exactly the right skills and attitudes God provides people He has designed to finish His work. A servant leader will need help, but always empower others to do and be what God has called them to do and be. Thank God right now for the special people God has given you to work with in His Kingdom. Jot down names and pray for them as Paul prayed for his co-workers in Philippians 1:3, 4,

> *"I thank my God upon every remembrance of you, always in every prayer of mine making request for you all with joy."*

People who know, develop and use their gifts as God directs are key to advancing the Kingdom of God on earth..

1.   6.
2.   7.
3.   8.
4.   9.
5.   10.

Resource number three

The third greatest resource is money. Ministry requires money. Supplies cost money. Tom Phillips of the Billy Graham Association says,

"One of the outstanding guiding tools God the Holy Spirit uses is funding. By beginning in prayer and having God the Holy Spirit to guide interested people who want to see such a ministry funded, the ministry usually gears according to God's provision."[41]

My Bible school teacher used to say,

"God's will is God's bill."

God will help you with financial resources and equipment needed to be a strategic servant leader.

Questions

1. What is God saying to you?_____
   _____
   _____

2. What people resources do you need? _____
   _____
   _____

3. What people are working with you? _____
   _____
   _____

4. What money and supply needs are essential to your ministry? _____
   _____
   _____

𝒶 STANDS FOR AIM

What is my general aim?

What am I aiming to do as a servant leader?

My aim as a servant leader is to:

> "...understand and desire the ability to marshal and steward resources over time to effectively carry out the significant task God has given me."[42]

Michael Hackman and Craig Johnson commented on one of Stephen Covey's *Seven Habits of Highly Effective People*,

> "'Put first things first.' This principle is based on the notion that a leader's time should be organized around priorities. Too many leaders spend their time coping with emergencies and neglecting long-range planning and relationships. They mistakenly believe that urgent items are always important. Effective leaders carve out time for significant activities by identifying their most important roles, selecting their goals, creating schedules that enable them to reach their objectives, and modifying their plans when

necessary. They also know how to delegate tasks and have the courage to say 'no' to requests that do not fit their priorities."[43]

The above information spotlights a broad or general aim. Next we will look at pinpointing the focus.

Questions

1. What is your general aim?_____

    _____

    _____

    _____

    _____

    _____

2. How are you doing toward stewarding your aim? _____

    _____

    _____

    _____

3. What are any distractions to completing the task? _____

    _____

    _____

    _____

    _____

    _____

    _____

    _____

$\mathcal{T}$ STANDS FOR TARGET

What is your specific target? How will you know what is most important? There are many questions to ask! Why? What? Where? When? Who? I believe if we answer the why question all the other questions fall into line. *Why* are we doing this? *What* is the end goal?

How is definitely the wrong question. Peter Block states his reflections on why:

> "There is depth in the question 'How do I do this?' that is worth exploring. The question is a defense against the action. It is a leap past the question of intentions, and past the drama of responsibility. The question 'How?' – more than any other question – looks for the answer outside ourselves. It is our indirect expression of our doubts – our search for the manual's recipes – the practical is endless."

Why are we doing this?

The nonfiction best-seller list is filled with recipe bits that have nothing to do with cooking.

> "I was with a group that wanted to know how to implement improvement and participation. Who doesn't? I asked the audience how many of them had read the books, *Thriving on Chaos*, *Seven Habits of Highly Effective People*, the *Empowered Manager* and *The Fifth Discipline*. Most of the group raised a hand.

In those four books there are over 925, count them, specific suggestions on how to move the workplace toward high-performing and customer-centered directions. If we have seen these books and others as more than enough practical suggestions we could possibly use in a lifetime, why are we still asking the questions 'How?' The experience of searching outside for answers expresses our doubts about being enough, having enough, doing enough."[44]

You get to help develop the *how*!

Why is the right question to hit the bull's eye on the target. Jesus knew why He came to earth. The disciples knew why they were told to "go into all the world."

Answer the why question and you will see your "arrow" hit the bull's eye!

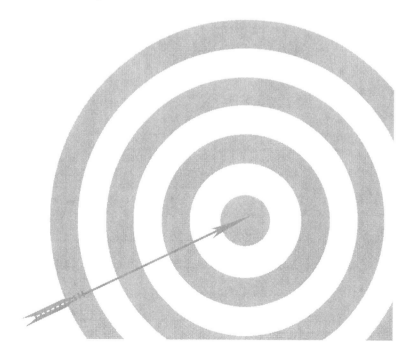

Questions

1. Why are you doing this? _____

   _____

   _____

   _____

   _____

   _____

   _____

   _____

   _____

   _____

   _____

2. What *is* the target? _____

   _____

   _____

   _____

   _____

   _____

   _____

   _____

   _____

   _____

   _____

   _____

   _____

   _____

E STANDS FOR EVALUATION

As a servant leader who wants to be strategic, it is important to evaluate yourself. It is also important to evaluate the ministry in which you are involved.

Questions

1. What needs to stop? List anything in your personal ministry or the church that is wasting your time and needs to stop. _____

    _____

    _____

    _____

    _____

    _____

2. What needs to start? Is there something new and innovative that would help your servant leadership? _____

    _____

    _____

    _____

    _____

    _____

    _____

3. How are people doing? Are the people with whom you work tired, happy, frustrated, directionless, effective, etc.?_____

    _____

It is important to evaluate yourself.

4. Are there changes needed? What are they? __

   _____

   _____

   _____

   _____

   _____

5. What is going well? _____

   _____

   _____

   _____

   _____

   _____

   _____

6. What makes you feel good?_____

   _____

   _____

   _____

   _____

   _____

   _____

7. What is God blessing right now?_____

   _____

   _____

   _____

   _____

   _____

   _____

   _____

𝒢 STANDS FOR GOALS

As a strategic servant leader it is necessary to have goals.

"In essence the path-goal theory of leadership 'is about how leaders motivate subordinates to accomplish designated goals' (Northouse 2010). Subordinates are restricted by their leaders to achieve these goals when leaders clearly define the goals, clarify the path to completing their goals, remove obstacles to completing the goals, and provide support to help achieve pre-assigned goals (Northouse, 2010)."[45]

In Philippians 3:10-12, Paul says,

"...that I may know Him and the power of His resurrection, and the fellowship of His sufferings, being conformed to His death, if, by any means, I may attain to the resurrection from the dead. Not that I have already attained, or am already perfected; but I press on, that I may lay hold of that for which Christ Jesus has also laid hold of me."

Paul had personal goals to know Christ, to know the power of His resurrection, and the fellowship of His suffering. He wanted to lay hold of what God had laid hold of him for – so He pressed on to that work by forgetting what was past and reaching for the goal!

...it is necessary to have goals.

What are your personal goals?

Setting goals does many things. Below are four helps when setting goals.

Goals keep us:

1. Focused
2. Able to measure what we are doing
3. Taking ownership to reach them
4. Able to celebrate when the goal is reached

"Effective teams are clearly focused on goals that maximize team outcomes. Further, these goals inspire the team to perform at peak levels."[46]

First, goal setting gives us a focus. Jesus had a focus to go to the cross and rise again.

"From that time Jesus began to show His disciples that He must go to Jerusalem, and suffer many things from the elders, chief priests and scribes, be killed and be raised the third day. Then Peter took Him aside and began to rebuke Him, saying, 'Far be it from You, Lord, this shall not happen to You!'

But He turned and said to Peter, 'Get behind Me, Satan! You are an offense to Me, for you are not mindful of the things of God, but the things of men.'"[47]

Jesus was focused on His goal

Second, goal setting helps measure progress toward the goal. It sets a mark to reach. In Proverbs 29:18 it says,

"Where there is no vision, the people perish."

Or as George Barna puts it,

"You need a plan, complete with goals, strategies and tactics, to move forward effectively, and efficiently. You need to create processes to introduce the vision into ministry in practical ways. You may have evaluative tools prepared so you can assess how well you are doing along the way, fine-tuning your implementation efforts as you go along."[48]

Third, goal setting requires ownership of the task. You know what direction to take. Even in their goal in Acts 1:8, the disciples received power to be witnesses in Jerusalem, Judea and Samaria and the outermost parts of the world. They owned it, then did it.

Fourth, goal setting gives us cause to celebrate. Often the church and ministries in the Kingdom of God are not good at celebrating victories except at Christmas and Easter. You can thank your co-laborers, appreciate them in a tangible way, and celebrate their accomplishments.

...goal setting requires ownership of the task.

What is

this

year's

emphasis?

Questions

1. Have you set goals? _____

   _____

   _____

   _____

2. How are you doing with goal completion? ____

   _____

   _____

   _____

   _____

3. Have you been celebrating your co-laborers
   when they achieve something? _____

   _____

   _____

   _____

   _____

Y STANDS FOR YEAR

I have emphasized, "What is God saying?" I now will

ask, "What is the year's emphasis?"

In Ecclesiastes 3:1-8 Solomon writes:

"To everything there is a season,

A time for every purpose under heaven:

A time to be born,

And a time to die:

A time to plant,

And a time to pluck what is planted;

A time to kill,

And a time to heal;

A time to break down,

And a time to build up;

A time to weep,

And a time to laugh;

A time to mourn,

And a time to dance;

A time to cast away stones,

And a time to gather stones;

A time to embrace,

And a time to refrain from embracing;

A time to gain,

And a time to lose;

A time to keep,

And a time to throw away;

A time to tear,

And a time to sew;

A time to keep silence,

And a time to speak;

A time to love,

And a time to hate;

A time of war,

And a time of peace."

It says in this passage that there is a time for every purpose under heaven. What should you emphasize in order to reach your intended goal?

I also ask you, "What season are we in?" What is God doing all around us? Let's follow His lead! Ken Blanchard and Phil Hodges say it well,

> "Servant leadership starts with a vision and ends with a servant heart that helps people live according to that vision."[49]

Part of servant leadership is to be a *strategic* leader. Watch God give you strategies just as He gave them to Jehoshaphat in II Chronicles 20 or Moses in Exodus 17. Look it up – GOD IS AWESOME!

Chapter Four

SHEPHERD LEADERSHIP

As you may recall, at the beginning of this workbook I said the Lord spoke to my heart out of Psalm 78:70-72:

> *"He also chose David His servant, and took him from the sheepfolds; from following the ewes that had young He brought him, to shepherd Jacob His people, and Israel His inheritance. So he shepherded them according to the integrity of his heart, and guided them by the skillfulness of his hands."*

God called me back to graduate school to develop "the skillfulness of my hands." This will help me give the people I lead more effective leadership tools for their ministry. David as a shepherd and leader, *"shepherded them according to the integrity of his heart."* His shepherding experience prepared him to be the king and leader of Jacob, God's people and Israel, God's inheritance.

Part of being a servant leader is to be a shepherd of people. A biblical leader or pastor is seen as a shepherd of a flock of sheep. Proverbs 27:23 says,

> *"Be diligent to know the state of your flocks, and attend to your herds."*

...be a shepherd of the people.

In other words, it is important to know if the people you lead are doing well. Someone has said, "A shepherd smells like sheep."

Here is an acrostic for S-H-E-P-H-E-R-D:

S STANDS FOR SHEEP

A shepherd cares for his sheep. As a shepherd leader we need to know our people and their needs.

> *"A shepherd knows each sheep by name; he nurtures the young, bandages the wounded, cares for the weak, and protects them all."[50]*

Psalm 23 tells us:

> *"The Lord is my shepherd;*
> *I shall not want.*
> *He makes me to lie down in green pastures;*
> *He leads me beside the still waters.*
> *He restores my soul;*
> *He leads me in the paths of righteousness*
> *For His name's sake.*
> *Yes, though I walk through the valley of the shadow*
> *of death,*
> *I will fear no evil;*
> *For You are with me;*
> *Your rod and Your staff, they comfort me.*

...a shepherd smells like sheep.

You prepare a table before me in the presence

of my enemies;

You anoint my head with oil;

My cup runs over.

Surely goodness and mercy shall follow me

All the days of my life;

And I will dwell in the house of the Lord forever."

The Lord is my shepherd

It is important for every shepherd leader to personally know the Lord as their shepherd. He will be there to care for you as you lead others. In Psalm 23 we see the one who is shepherded by the Lord shall not want. This means that we each know the Good Shepherd.

In John 10:14 it says,

"I am the good shepherd; and I know My sheep, and am known by my own."

Depend on the Good Shepherd as you shepherd others. By using Psalm 23 as a handbook, we see that we can follow the Good Shepherd's example by leading and guiding those we shepherd. We can work with the Good Shepherd to lead the sheep. He leads us and we can work with Him to lead people to green pastures and to be beside still waters (v. 2).

Ezekiel 34:14 says,

'I will feed them in good measure, and their fold shall be on the high mountains of Israel. There they shall lie down in a good fold and feed in rich pasture on the mountains of Israel."

Question

What is the state of those you lead? _____

_____

_____

_____

_____

ℋ STANDS FOR HEALS

The shepherd leader as healer

A shepherd leader should bring healing to the people (sheep) they lead. People in ministry and leadership positions can be hurt and wounded and need healing.

In Psalm 23:5 it states,

"...You anoint my head with oil; My cup runs over."

Phillip Keller explains the anointing, "I always preferred to use a homemade remedy composed of linseed oil, sulphur and tar which was smeared over the sheep's nose and head as a protection against nose flies."[51]

The anointing oil brought protection and healing to the sheep. It soothed their scabs and stopped the spread of infectious diseases. In Isaiah 61 it says Jesus was anointed with oil to bind up the brokenhearted. God wants to use us to speak healing and minister healing to those we lead.

Shepherd leaders go after their strays

Ezekiel 34:11-14 states:

> "For thus says the Lord God, 'Indeed I Myself will search for My sheep and seek them out. As a shepherd seeks out his flock on the day he is among his scattered sheep, so will I seek out My sheep and deliver them from all the places where they were scattered on a cloudy and dark day. And I will bring them out from the peoples and gather them from the countries and will bring them to their own land; I will feed them on the mountains of Israel, in the valleys and in all the inhabited places of the country.'"

It is necessary to go after sheep that are scattered and have been hurt. The heart of the shepherd leader is to bring those that are scattered back where they belong. The heart of a shepherd is to keep the flock safe from predators by keeping them together. Because of life's dilemmas, at

God wants to use us to speak healing and minister healing to those we lead.

times people you lead will be tempted to run and not be able to face different challenges. This is when the shepherd leader needs to follow up on those who are "missing in action."

In Ezekiel 34:16 the Lord says,

> *"I will seek what was lost and bring back what is driven away, bind up the broken and strengthen what was sick, but I will destroy the fat and the strong, and feed them in judgment."*

God help us to seek the sheep that are lost.

Question

Do I know of hurting or scattered sheep in my charge who need God's touch? _____

_____

_____

_____

$\mathcal{E}$ STANDS FOR EQUIP

A shepherd leader equips the saints

Ephesians 4:11-16 says:

> *"And He Himself gave some to be apostles, some prophets, some evangelists and some pastors and teachers,*

for the equipping of the saints for the work of ministry, for the edifying of the body of Christ till we all come to the unity of the faith and of the knowledge of the Son of God, to a perfect man, to the measure of the stature of the fullness of Christ; that we should no longer be children, tossed to and fro and carried about with every wind of doctrine by the trickery of men, in the cunning craftiness of deceitful plotting, but, speaking the truth in love, may grow up in all things into Him who is the head – Christ – from whom the whole body, joined and knit together by what every joint supplies according to the effective working by which every part does its share, causes growth of the body for the edifying of itself in love."

As we equip the people we serve, we find out where they are placed in the Body of Christ and the Kingdom of God. I have found when a person discovers how they are gifted and their calling, they begin to grow and find focus. When we know a person's calling and gifting, we can help them develop.

In I Corinthians 12:1, Paul said,

"Now concerning spiritual gifts, brethren, I do not want you to be ignorant."

...when a person discovers how they are gifted and their calling, they begin to grow and find focus.

We have all been set in the body as it pleases God.

I Corinthians 12:18 says,

> *"But now God has set the members, each one of them, in the body just as He pleased."*

Each person wants to know "their" place.

A shepherd leader sees the gifts

If we are ineffective as a shepherd leader in equipping and placing people, we will hinder their growth. Helping people discover their heart, gifts and callings helps them find their place in life.

> "Apart from the acquisition of general leadership skills, the most important development during the middle-sum-phase of the Ministry Maturity phase involves discovering spiritual gifts and using them confidently. A spiritual gift is a unique capacity for channeling the Holy Spirit power into a ministry."[52]

Clinton also noticed two aspects of discovering your gifts: like attracts like and giftedness vs. drift. The table on the following page shows his thoughts on the matter:

Pattern	Explanation
Like attracts like	Potential leaders are intuitively attracted to leaders who have the same spiritual gifts.
Gifted vs. drift	Potential leaders respond intuitively to ministry challenges and assignments that call for their spiritual gifts, even if not explicitly knowing.[53]

Question

How are you equipping your entrusted "sheep"?

_____

_____

_____

_____

$\mathcal{P}$ STANDS FOR PASTOR-TEACHER

Shepherds are pastor-teachers

A servant leader that is a shepherd leader is a pastor-teacher. In Ephesians 4:14-16 it says that some are called to be pastors and teachers to equip the saints and to bring them to a place of maturity. A pastor-teacher cares for the needs of others.

"Leadership is first a spiritual matter of the heart. Whenever you have an opportunity or responsibility to influence the thinking and the behavior of

A pastor-teacher cares for the needs of others.

others, the first choice you are called to make is whether to be motivated by self-interest or by the benefit of those you are leading. The heart- question that Jesus asks is, 'Are you a servant leader or a self-serving leader?'"[54]

The heart of Jesus was that of a pastor (Good Shepherd) and a teacher (Master Teacher). In leading others for their benefit, we do some pastoring and some teaching.

Psalm 23 nuggets

There are two passages of Scripture that speak to that area of leadership.

In Psalm 23:2 it says,

> *"He restores my soul; He leads me in the paths of righteousness for His name's sake."*

There are two things a pastor-teacher will be involved in while doing servant leadership.

A servant leader should be involved in leading their sheep beside the still waters. We need to lead people to the places of refreshing for their lives. *"He leads me beside still water."*

> "Jesus is the one who gives us the water of eternal life and refreshing of the Holy Spirit for the Lamb who

is in the midst of the throne will shepherd them and lead them to the fountain of living water."[55]

People we serve need to be shepherded.

Integrity

A servant leader also should lead people in paths of righteousness for God's name sake. Integrity is an integral part of walking in paths of righteousness.

Proverbs 11:3 says,

> "The integrity of the upright will guide them, but the perversity of the unfaithful will destroy them."

Integrity gives us guidance

Integrity will guide you to know which path is righteous and which is unrighteous.

> "The God-given capacity to lead has two parts: giftedness and character. Integrity is the heart of character."[56]

Integrity is essential to walking in righteousness.

> "There are three parts to an integrity check: the challenge to consistency with inner convictions, the response to the challenge and the resulting expansion of ministry."[57]

Integrity is an integral part of walking in paths of righteousness.

Joseph, Daniel, Moses, Mary and Joseph passed integrity tests. God help us walk in righteous paths and direct others to do it as well.

Questions

1. Do you have an integrity test? OR What was the last one you had?_____

    _____

    _____

    _____

    _____

    _____

2. Of those you are leading, is there someone you could shepherd more effectively? _____

    _____

    _____

    _____

    _____

3. What must you teach to those you are leading?

    _____

    _____

    _____

    _____

    _____

    _____

H STANDS FOR HELPS

Help by mentoring

A shepherd leader is a helper. God helps us. We help others. We sometimes help by just being there for them. Everyone needs help.

One great way we can help is by mentoring. I developed a mentoring training course called *Equipmentor* which helps people find their *Personal Destiny, Personal Development, Personal Discipleship* and *Personal Deployment.* It has been amazing to watch my students grow spiritually. Pouring into them has been one of my greatest joys in the last few years.

Recently, mentoring has become very popular.

> "It really is an ancient concept, however, one exemplified by the wise, elder guide who helps a younger protégé along the journey. Joshua had Moses as his mentor. Elisha had Elijah. Timothy had Paul."[58]

Young people in particular are looking for mentors. I have been mentoring a number of people over the last few years – young and old. But particularly I have seen a growing interest in young men and women to have a mentor.

Young people in particular are looking for mentors.

"We have found that most younger leaders are hungry for an older person who will simply be available and interested, providing a listening ear and an understanding heart and whatever counsel the person can give from his own experience and knowledge of God, life and people."[59]

It is important to remember that *more is caught than taught*. Taking people with you as you do ministry and life is one of your best training tools. I have taken many people on mission and ministry trips and most of them have told me the tremendous impact it had on their lives. **TAKE PEOPLE WITH YOU WHERE GOD SENDS YOU AND THEN *SEND* THEM *OUT TO DO IT*!**

In John 20:21, Jesus said,

"So Jesus said to them again, 'Peace to you! As the Father has sent Me, I do also send you.'"

Help by being there

Many times I find just by "being there" we help people.

Many times I find just by "being there" we help people. Sometimes people just want to know somebody is in their corner in the fight of life.

Paul had that in Epaphroditus in Philippians 2:25-30:

"Yet I consider it necessary to send you to Epaphroditus my brother, fellow worker and fellow soldier, but your

messenger and the one who ministered to my need; since he was longing for you all, and was distressed because you had heard that he was sick. For indeed he was sick almost unto death; but God had mercy on him, and not only on him but on me also, lest I should have sorrow upon sorrow. Therefore I send him the more eagerly, that when you see him again you may rejoice, and I may be less sorrowful. Receive him therefore in the Lord with all gladness and hold such men in esteem; because for the work of Christ he came close to death, not regarding his life, to supply what was lacking in your service toward me."

Epaphroditus almost died just to be there with Paul while he was in prison. Paul said this is the type of man you should hold in high esteem.

Questions

1. Is there someone you are mentoring under your shepherd's care? _____

   _____

   _____

2. Who needs you just to be with them right now just as Epaphroditus was with Paul? _____

   _____

   _____

   _____

E STANDS FOR ENCOURAGE

Encourage: put courage into them

A servant leader should be encouraging the sheep they lead. To encourage someone is to put courage into them. To discourage someone is to take courage out of them. Let's put courage into the people we are serving for the Lord.

In order to encourage someone, it is important to see their potential. God sees the potential in people. He saw Saul of Tarsus as the Apostle Paul. He saw Sarai as Sarah the Mother of Many Nations. He saw Abram as Abraham, the Father of Many Nations. He saw Simon as the Apostle Peter to Israel. He sees the potential in you and others. A good athletic coach sees the potential in his players and works to develop it.

W. Glenn Rowe and Laura Guerrero from *Cases in Leadership*, listed below are ten Cs on how to engage employee's heads, hearts and hands:

1. Connect – Caring relationship
2. Career – Career achievement
3. Clarity – Clear vision
4. Convey – Convey expectations
5. Congratulate – Congratulate wins
6. Contribute – Contribute impact

> In order to encourage someone, it is important to see their potential.

7.   Control – Control for employee

8.   Collaborate – Good teams

9.   Credibility – Credible ethic and reputation

10. Confidence – Create confidence

These are some things to remember as you encourage (put courage into) your team. People respond well to encouragement. I remember when I was coaching a young boys' basketball team and one of the fathers said, "I need to talk to you about what my son said about you." I thought, "Oh, no, what did I do?" But in quoting his son, the father said, "Dad, I like this coach. When we do something wrong, he just shows us how to do it right." We can help people when things go wrong "by just showing them how to do it right."

Motivate

Motivation has much to do with empowerment.
We are to be empowering the people we serve.
God has empowered us!

"For each of us as individuals, empowerment means placing ourselves in the position of being creators of the organization to which we belong. Empowerment is embodied in the act of standing our ground, discovering our own voice, making our own choices, regardless of the level of power and privilege we hold.

It stems from our choice of the mindset that tells us that we have within ourselves the authority to act and to speak and to serve clients and those around us. We do not need permission to take what matters into our own hands."[60]

Motivate people to be empowered to grow and develop as an individual and as part of a team.

Believe in them

Leaders must make followers feel needed.

People flourish when their leaders believe in them. "Leaders must make followers feel needed."[61] This is because they *are* needed. I want to develop leaders of leaders more than I want to develop leaders of followers.

As we look at the model of Jesus, He trusted His followers to become leaders. His actions showed He believed in them.

"Jesus trusted them. At the very beginning, He told them to follow Him, then taught them by letting them live with Him and watch Him. He sent them out to go and to do, entrusting them with a task. Jesus shows us that leaders are made not just by telling them what to do, but also trusting them to do it."[62]

In Hebrews 10:23-25 it reads,

"Let us hold fast the confession of our hope without wavering, for He who promised is faithful. And let us consider one another in order to stir up love and good works, not forsaking the assembling of ourselves together, as is the manner of some, but exhorting one another, and so much the more as you see the Day approaching."

R STANDS FOR RESTORES

Soul restoration

A shepherd leader is involved in the ministry of restoration. As we walk with people we will see that many need restoration in different parts of their lives.

In Psalm 23:3 it says,

"He restores my soul…"

God is in the restoration business

The word restore means, "to return to a former condition or position."[63]

He wants to restore people's souls – their mind, will and emotions. He wants us to help others be refreshed and restored.

...it is vital to build relationships as you work with people.

Recharge your batteries

When our batteries are low, we need recharging. Working with pastors and ministry leaders, I see that many are workaholics, or should I say "ministryholics." They often need someone to help with their schedules. Part of the task I see is how we can refresh and restore ministry leaders in the midst of life. Spiritual warfare and pressures are forced daily on ministry leaders.

Every person is unique. It is vital that you find out what replenishes them and make sure they do it. God says your table is ready! In Psalm 23:5, David said,

"You prepare a table before me in the presence of my enemies."

One of the ways God prepares a table is to allow a leader to help prepare His table. We are to be under-shepherds to the Good Shepherd, Jesus. It is necessary to work with Him as "He is setting the table" for the people we mentor in ministry. God wants us to help restore relationships to Him and others because some people we shepherd need to be restored.

In ministry it is vital to build relationships as you work with people. One of the ways to help "set a table" during their times of unmet expectations is to encourage people to "stay the course." Discouragement can easily persuade a person to quit.

"Proverbs 13:12 describes the pain of unfulfilled expectations, 'Hope deferred makes the heart sick…' As the writer of this proverb, many leaders have experienced the pain of longing for something that forever seems out of reach. We know the pain of hard work toward a goal that is never actualized. I have thought we expressed our needs and expectations, but they were ignored, dismissed or outright defied."[64]

It is helpful to let your people know part of the journey with Christ takes time to develop.

Questions

1. In your ministry who needs to be restored? __

   _____

   _____

   _____

   _____

   _____

2. In the midst of the battle do you need to help "set a table" for someone? _____

   _____

   _____

   _____

   _____

   _____

   _____

   _____

$\mathcal{D}$ STANDS FOR DISCIPLES

Disciples the goal

As a shepherd leader, our goal is for the sheep to be disciples of Jesus Christ. Matthew 28:18-20 says,

> "And Jesus came and spoke to them, saying, 'All authority has been given to Me in heaven and on earth. Go therefore and make disciples of all the nations, baptizing them in the name of the Father and of the Son and of the Holy Spirit, teaching them to observe all things that I have commanded you; and lo, I am with you always, even to the end of the age. Amen."

Teaching leaders takes time and effort.

Our goal should make disciples that are baptized and trained to observe all they are commanded to do.

To disciple someone means to spend time with them, love them, preach, teach and release them to their call. Teaching leaders of leaders takes time and effort.

In John 13:35 Jesus said,

> "By this all will know that you are My disciples, if you have love for one another."

How do Christians or disciples of Jesus see themselves?

> "But among themselves, the preferred term for disciples was followers of Jesus or followers of the Way.

John the Baptist had prepared 'the way of the Lord.'
Jesus had constituted his disciples with two decisive
words: 'Follow me.' So there was no 'Christianity'
abroad on the earth, only a radical, new 'Way' and a
motley band of 'brothers' and 'sisters' who were 'followers of the Way.'"[65]

Simply put, a disciple is a "follower of Jesus Christ as Lord."

Disciples sent

Our goal as a shepherd leader is to see disciples sent to finish the work they have been given to do.

It was said by Jesus in John 17:4,

> *"I have glorified You on the earth. I have finished the
> work which You have given Me to do."*

This is the model of Jesus

> "The Shepherd and flock relationship eloquently
> implies at least three qualities of spiritual leadership:
> availability, commitment and trust. This is how spiri-
> tual flocks are formed today."[66]

These are all needed to make disciples and send them to
their work. A true biblical leader is a shepherd leader who
cares for people.

Questions

1. Whom are you discipling?_____

   _____

   _____

   _____

   _____

   _____

   _____

   _____

2. Do you know the work they are sent to do? __

   _____

   _____

   _____

   _____

   _____

   _____

3. Do you smell like sheep?_____

   _____

   _____

   _____

   _____

   _____

   _____

   _____

REMEMBER:

<u>S</u>heep

<u>H</u>eals

<u>E</u>quips

<u>P</u>astors-Teaches

<u>H</u>elps

<u>E</u>ncourages

<u>R</u>estores

<u>D</u>isciples

"Leadership involves caring."

Conclusion

A shepherd leader cares for their sheep. Leadership involves caring. God can give us insight to guide His sheep. Having an attitude of a shepherd to protect, heal, encourage and restore will yield huge dividends.

Chapter Five

SITUATIONAL LEADERSHIP

I want to look at situational leadership for the servant leader in areas of Christian ministry: change and conflict. These are two things that ministry leaders deal with constantly. Often they have not been adequately equipped to know what to do during change or conflict. What is situational leadership?

"The situational leadership theory has two underlying assumptions. First, as situations vary, so must a person's leadership. This means that leaders are able to adopt their styles to different situations. Second, leadership is made up of a directive component and a supportive component, and these two components have to be exercised appropriately based on the context. To assess the appropriate level of each component, it is critical that leaders evaluate their subordinates and determine their level of competence and commitment to a given task or job."[67]

Rowe and Guerrero go on to state that,

"There are four styles of leadership to use in situational leadership: Directing Leadership style, Coaching Leadership style, Supporting Leadership style, and Delegating Leadership style.

When situations arise, it is important to know your leaders and especially how your whole team works together.

Situational leadership styles

The Directing Leadership style should be used in situations where the subordinate does not know what to do in a given circumstance. The leader will need to be direct and give instructions. This is often used for people who are new or developing new skills.

The Coaching Leadership style should be used when the situation calls for high direction and high support. Often this style is used when the conditions call for constructive and social support for the subordinate.

The Supporting Leadership style is used when the subordinate has the skills and does not so much need direction. But what the subordinate needs is support if there is a problem or just needs encouragement.

The Delegating Leadership style is used when employees are confident and skilled. This type of person can get the job done by themselves with their team."[68]

When situations arise, it is important to know your leaders and especially how your whole team works together.

"A leader is not always successful in every situation. A leader's effectiveness depends on his or her personality, the behavior of followers, the nature of the task, and many other situational factors."[69]

For many pastors and Christian leaders two areas stand out for situational leadership issues: change and conflict.

Change

We live in a changing, complex culture in the twenty-first century. Change affects the church.

> "Leadership is different in a period of change. The leader must simultaneously deal with followers who are destabilized by change and resistant to it, and followers who are energized by change and eager for it. Many churches have both kinds of people."[70]

Change dynamics

The more we understand change, the easier it is to deal with it. Ken Blanchard and Phil Hodges state,

> "A key role servant leaders often play is facilitating necessary changes. As a result, it is imperative that these leaders recognize there are four levels that range in varying degrees of difficulty and time required: (1) knowledge; (2) attitude; (3) behavior, and (4) organizational change."[71]

Level One: Knowledge

The first dynamic of change is knowledge. During times of change educate people through different resources.

Change affects the church.

Use discussions, related books on the subject, classes, the assistance of experienced "experts" and encourage people on your team to study the Bible.

Level Two: Attitude

People are often emotional about different things when change takes place. Their position or program or the way they have always done things will be different. Many people do not like to change, since the world is constantly changing. People prefer to be comfortable rather than conformable.

Proverbs is full of practical attitudes that can help servant leaders and, when followed, connect a team together.

Proverbs 10:12, *"Hatred stirs up strife, But love covers all sins."*

Proverbs 10:14, *"Wise people store up knowledge, But the mouth of the foolish is near destruction."*

Proverbs 11:2, 3, *"When pride comes, then comes shame; But with the humble is wisdom. The integrity of the upright will guide them, But the perversity of the unfaithful will destroy them."*

Proverbs 11:14, *"Where there is no counsel, the people fall; But in the multitude of counselors there is safety."*

Proverbs 11:27, *"He who earnestly seeks good finds favor, but trouble will come to him who seeks evil."*

Proverbs 12:25, *"Anxiety in the heart of man causes depression, but a good word makes it glad."*

Proverbs 26:20, *"Where there is no wood, the fire goes out; and where there is no talebearer, strife ceases."*

These verses show attitudes of: love, openness to learn, humility, openness to counsel, seeking the good of God and people, speaking good words and not being a talebearer (gossip and slanderer). These attitudes will help team members keep a right heart during change.

Level Three: Behavior

Behavior comes out of what we believe about ourselves and others. Behavior that becomes habit is hard to break. Sometimes it is more beneficial to help change a belief system before trying to change behavior.

Helping people understand how God views others in Christ Jesus can help change their behavior.

Level Four: Organizational Change

Organizational change is different from individual change. The dynamics of change to influence a group vs. an individual can be a much bigger task. How can we help each other through change?

Behavior comes out of what we believe about ourselves and others.

Helpful hints during change

Thinking of change, I have found a few things that can help people flow through it.

First, find out what people are feeling – there can be many different feelings.

Second, help people realize we are all in this together and need to help each other. Also, help people grieve their losses and talk about what they are losing. Then help people prioritize steps to take during the change.

Some questions to ask might be the following:

Why are we doing this?

What is most important?

If you help people believe that God will guide them through the change, it will make changing easier. Remember, without leadership people tend to do things in their old ways. Do you remember Peter and the disciples? When Jesus died they went back to their old, familiar ways – fishing. That is what Jesus told them to leave when they first followed Him.

There will be as many different responses to change as there are people on your team. The most effective change happens through relationship.

I once heard someone say, "It is important to signal before you change lanes." We all probably have led or been involved in a change where it felt as if you went from the slow lane to the express lane without anyone signaling. In the gospels Jesus was continually telling His disciples about changes that would be coming concerning His death and resurrection. He "signaled before He changed lanes." May God help us seek His wisdom whenever we as servant leaders must negotiate the course.

Questions

1. What changes are you personally experiencing and how are you handling them? _____
   _____
   _____
   _____
   _____

2. What changes are corporately being made and how are you handling them?_____
   _____
   _____
   _____

3. How are others around you responding to the changes? _____
   _____
   _____
   _____

...signal before you change lanes.

Conflict

Conflict is part of life. Some handle it better than others. As servant leaders in the Kingdom of God, we will surely have situations where we need to deal with conflict.

"Conflict does not have to be unhealthy. It is a natural result of working together. Conflict is a test for us, often resulting from two different perspectives which derive from our different personalities, depending on how we are wired. Some of us welcome conflict and confrontation. Others run from it."[72]

Different responses to conflict

I have found three basic responses to conflict:

- Those who run away from it
- Those who run toward it
- Those who reconcile in the midst of it

Some people run from conflict

Some people run away from conflict because of past hurts or fear of how people will react towards them. I have realized over the last 32 years of being a pastor that if you do not confront problems, they do not go away. You will run into them again…and again…and again.

Some people run toward conflict

Some people love conflict. This type of person tends to bowl others over and make them do what they want by sheer force of personality.

In the long run, control is not healthy for relationships and team building. Every person's heart and feelings need to be valued. In the early 1930s, Elton Mayo of Harvard University researched and studied people who were following in his footsteps. He determined that,

> "The most significant factor affecting organizational productivity was … interpersonal relationships that we developed on the job."[73]

Helping build healthy relationships is vital to a team's productivity.

Some people like to bring reconciliation between God and others

Some like to help people through conflict and confrontation toward healthy relationships. In Matthew 5:9 Jesus said,

> *"Blessed are the peacemakers, for they shall be called sons of God."*

A child of God wants to help make peace between people and God. They also want to bring reconciliation to human relationships. Many reconcilers have learned when to give advice and when not to give it. They have also learned to help each of those involved take responsibility for their part in causing the conflict. This provides hope for those people involved that God will bring good out of conflict.

Conflict is inevitable. Though it might seem difficult, it is a tool God uses to bring change and growth in our lives. Larry Kreider put it well,

> "Healthy working relationships will encourage the members to air their opinions freely and openly. Disagreements are an opportunity to demonstrate understanding, respect, and acceptance of others, thus strengthening results. Conflict allows us to recognize our deficiencies, and invite the Lord to convert them as we grow spiritually."[74]

Jesus' method of dealing with conflict in relationships

In Matthew 7:1-6 God says:

> *"Judge not, that you be not judged. For with what judgment you judge, you will be judged; and with the measure you use, it will be measured back to you.*
>
> *And why do you look at the speck in your brother's eye, but do not consider the plank in your own eye? Or how can you say to your brother, "Let me remove the speck from your eye;" and look a plank is in your own eye?*

Conflict is inevitable.

Hypocrite! First remove the plank from your own eye, and then you will see clearly to remove the speck from your brother's eye. Do not give what is holy to the dogs nor cast your pearls before swine, lest they trample them under their feet, and turn and tear you in pieces."

And Matthew 18:15-17 says,

"Moreover if your brother sins against you, go and tell him his fault between you and him alone. If he hears you, you have gained your brother. But if he will not hear; take with you one or two more, that by the mouth of two or three witnesses every word may be established. And if he refuses to hear them, tell it to the church. But if he refuses even to hear the church, let him be to you like a heathen and a tax collector."

Four basic conflict principles from Matthew 18:15-17:

1. Glorify God by obeying His word. Go privately first; if needed take with you one or two more, and if needed take it to the church leadership.

2. Get the plank out of your own eye.

3. Go remove the speck from your brother's eye.

4. Be reconciled. Do you want to be right or do you want to be reconciled? Keep a right heart and attitude as you go to reconcile with someone.

> Do you want to be right or do you want to be reconciled?

Ephesians 4:32 says,

"And be kind to one another, tenderhearted, forgiving one another even as God in Christ forgave you." Follow the example of Jesus and His Word.

Questions

1. Is there conflict between you and anyone that needs to be reconciled? _____

   _____

2. Do you run away from conflict, run toward conflict, or seek to reconcile in the midst of conflict? _____

   _____

3. As a servant leader what areas do you need to improve in any given situation? _____

   _____

   _____

   _____

4. Is unresolved conflict affecting your team?____

   _____

   _____

   _____

5. How can the conflict you are experiencing help you and your team grow? _____

   _____

   _____

Chapter Six

SACRIFICIAL LEADERSHIP

Part of being a servant leader is having a willingness to make sacrifices for King Jesus and His Kingdom. Sacrificial leadership is very important to Christian leadership. The sacrifice is worth the reward of pleasing God and affecting others. It costs to be a servant leader for the Lord.

In Matthew 16:24-28, it says,

> *"Then Jesus said to His disciples, 'If anyone desires to come after Me, let him deny himself, and take up his cross, and follow Me. For whoever desires to save his life will lose it, but whoever loses his life for My sake will find it. For what profit is it to a man if he gains the whole world and loses his own soul? Or what will a man give in exchange for his soul? For the Son of Man will come in the glory of His Father with His angels, and then He will reward each according to his works. Assuredly, I say to you, there are some standing here who shall not taste death till they see the Son of Man coming in His kingdom.'"*

Denying ourselves and taking up our cross to follow Jesus is part of being His disciple. If we lose our life for His sake, we will find our life. In biblical times, a disciple was a follower of Jesus Christ.

It costs to be a servant leader for the Lord.

"Christianity without discipleship is always Christianity without Christ."[75]

We are to be disciples (followers) of Jesus Christ.

The cost of discipleship demands one's willingness to leave all things behind and follow Jesus wherever he leads. Cheap grace serves as discipleship's bitterest foe, which true discipleship must loathe. Cheap grace is our enemy because it makes a life of transformation optional. Bonhoeffer said, 'We must never make cheap what was costly to God." No tepid responses to what cost everything to Christ! Our response should be discipleship – our lives, our all."[76]

Any cost we "pay" to be His disciple is worth the reward to know that we do it out of love for Him. Jesus gave His all; we must too!

We will look at sacrificial leadership in this workbook. We will use the following acrostic: C-O-S-T. It will cost you to follow Jesus!

C STANDS FOR COUNT THE COST

God's ultimate desire is for us to become Christlike. In Romans 8:28-30, we read:

"And we know that all things work together for good to those who love God, to those who are the called

according to His purpose. For whom He foreknew,
He also predestined to be conformed to the image of
His Son, that He might be the firstborn among many
brethren. Moreover whom He predestined, these He
also called; whom He called, these He also justified;
and whom He justified, these He also glorified."

I have heard the story many times that a refiner refines silver until he can see his reflection in the crucible. God refines us like silver until He can see the reflection of His Son Jesus in us. We are all being conformed to the image of His Son. He has called us, justified us and is glorifying us according to Romans 8:30.

John Maxwell said, "A leader must give up to go up."[77]

Count the cost leader

For the servant leader, being a sacrificial leader is a lifetime commitment.

> One servant leader said, "Sacrifice is a constant in leadership. It is an ongoing process, not a one-time payment. When I look back at my cases, I recognize that there has always been a cost involved in moving forward."[78]

As we move forward in God we sacrifice for the cause of Christ. The reward is worth the cost. It is so important to persevere through trials to finish the work God has given us to do.

We signed up for life in more ways than one.

"As a leader, press on to receive and achieve, to fulfill what Jesus Christ has destined for you. It will not just happen. There must be a pressing on in the spirit to fulfill all that Christ has for you. It takes discipline. Discipline is what gets us up in the morning when our bodies say, 'I need sleep.' Discipline keeps us fasting when our stomachs cry for food. Discipline keeps our thoughts and emotions on track when circumstances around us would dictate otherwise. Remember what Paul said in I Corinthians 9:27,

> *'I discipline my body like an athlete, training it to do what it should. Otherwise, I fear that after preaching to others I myself might be disqualified.'*"[79]

Counting the cost involves being disciplined and persevering in our ministry. We signed up for life in more ways than one.

Part of sacrificial leadership— Loving those who might not love back

One part of sacrificial leadership is to love those who might not love you back.

Jesus in Matthew 5:43-48 tells us about loving as God the Father loves – it costs,

> *"You have heard that it was said, 'You shall love your neighbor and hate your enemy.' But I say to you, love*

your enemies, bless those who curse you, do good for those who hate you, and pray for those who spitefully use you and persecute you, that you may be sons of your Father in heaven; for He makes His sun rise on the evil and on the good, and sends rain on the just and on the unjust. For if you love those who love you, what reward have you? Do not even the tax collectors do the same? And if you greet your brethren only, what do you do more than others? Do not even the tax collectors do so? Therefore you shall be perfect, just as your Father in heaven is perfect."

Another passage Jesus talks about on this subject is found in Luke 14:25-33:

"Now great multitudes went with Him. And He turned and said to them, 'If anyone comes to Me and does not hate his father and mother, wife and children, brother and sisters, yes, and his own life also, he cannot be My disciples. And whoever does not bear his cross and come after Me cannot be My disciple. For which of you, intending to build a tower, does not sit down first and count the cost, whether he has enough to finish it – lest, after he has laid the foundation, and is not able to finish, all who see it begin to mock him, saying, 'This man began to build and was not able to finish.'
Or what king, going to make war against another king, does not sit down first and consider whether he is able

> *with ten thousand to meet him who comes against him with twenty thousand? Or else, while the other is still a great way off, he sends a delegation and asks conditions of peace. So likewise, whoever of you does not forsake all that he has cannot be My disciple."*

First, the one who is not willing to submit totally to His authority, even more than every earthly relationship, cannot be His disciple.

Second, the one who counts the cost of bearing their cross and following Jesus will be His disciple.

Third, the King came to build His Kingdom and as a disciple we must face the fact of the cost of building with Him; looking at the whole process of discipleship from beginning to end.

Part of the cost of sacrificial life— Giving your life away

A sacrificial leader will constantly be giving the life of Jesus away. I have learned that if you help someone else with their vision, God helps you with yours. Or as Michael Adams said,

> "When you lay your life down for others, they will lay their life down for you."[80]

If you help someone else with their vision, God helps you with yours.

John 15:12, 13 tells what Jesus said,

"This is My commandment, that you love one another
as I have loved you. Greater love has no one than this,
than to lay down one's life for his friends."

How do we lay down our lives for others? Any way God directs us to do it.

Questions

1. Have you counted the cost?_____

    _____

    _____

    _____

    _____

    _____

2. What will the reward be for you? _____

    _____

    _____

    _____

    _____

3. How are you taking up your cross and denying yourself to follow Jesus? _____

    _____

    _____

    _____

    _____

    _____

How do we lay down our lives for others? Any way God directs us to do it.

𝒪 STANDS FOR OPENNESS

Openness to God

I love what Psalm 62:8 says,

> *"Trust in Him at all times, you people; pour out your heart before Him; God is a refuge for us."*

As a sacrificial leader, it is important to have your heart open to God. God will be a refuge for us as we pour out our heart through trials and sacrifices.

In Philippians 3:10, Paul said,

> *"...that I may know Him and the power of His resurrection, and the fellowship of His suffering, being conformed to His death."*

We can open up to God the Son, because He has suffered as we have. He understands what we are going through. There is a fellowship or joint participation with His sufferings that draws us close to Him. Once, after a person accused me of teaching in a spirit of legalism and bondage, I went back to my office and felt sorry for myself. As I was speaking to the Lord about it, He spoke to my heart and said,

> "What do you pray every morning?" And I said,
> "Lord, that person hurt me!" He said again, "What do

you pray every morning?" And I said, "Philippians 3:10 – that I may know You and the power of Your resurrection, and the fellowship of Your sufferings, being conformed to Your death."

Then the Lord said, "Fellowship with My sufferings…"

"That's not what I meant when I was saying that prayer."

And the Lord spoke to my heart and said,

"To the degree you know the fellowship of my sufferings, you will know the power of my resurrection."

I never forgot the experience. Keep an open heart. As sacrificial leaders lay down their lives for Him and others God can speak in the midst of hurt and pain.

Openness to others

There are others on your journey with Christ who have suffered and sacrificed. You can learn much from their experiences. God will give you people in life to open your heart.

"Leaders with clear moral purpose are vulnerable – a gift of all true leaders to their followers. Moral purpose enables leaders to be vulnerable because it changes the rules of measurement. A clear moral purpose removes the ego from the game. It means that leaders no longer need to succeed on the terms that make some leaders intolerant, inaccessible, and insufferable. Vulnerable leaders are open to diversity of gifts from followers. They seek contrary opinion. They take every person seriously. They are strong enough to abandon themselves to the strength of others. We need each other."[81]

In II Corinthians 7:5, 6 Paul says,

"For indeed, when we came to Macedonia, our bodies had no rest, but we were troubled on every side. Outside were conflicts, inside were fears. Nevertheless God, who comforts the downcast, comforted us by the coming of Titus."

God used Titus and the news he brought to comfort Paul and those with him. Be open to others in your times of sacrifice and suffering.

Openness to change

In the middle of trials, suffering and sacrifice, we are changed. In II Corinthians 4:16-18 we are told:

"Therefore we do not lose heart. Even though our outward man is perishing, yet the inward man is being renewed day by day. For our light affliction, which is

In the midst of trials, suffering and sacrifice, we are changed.

but for a moment, is working for us a far more exceed-
ing and eternal weight of glory, while we do not look at
the things which are seen, but at the things which are
not seen. For the things which are seen are temporary,
but the things which are not seen are eternal."

Paul is saying our light affliction is but for a moment in the light of eternity. And it is working *for* us not against us! Something begins inside us in the midst of trials and suffering … we become more like Jesus. Let God work afflictions *for* you not against you. Be open … the sacrifice is worth it! Because the Apostle Paul was open to sacrifice, ultimately his life affected others..

In Timothy 4:1-8, Paul says,

"I charge you therefore before God and the Lord Jesus
Christ, who will judge the living and the dead at His
appearing and His kingdom: Preach the word! Be
ready in season and out of season. Convince, rebuke,
exhort, with all long-suffering and teaching. For the
time will come when they will not endure sound doc-
trine, but according to their own desires, because they
have itching ears, they will heap up for themselves
teachers; and they will turn their ears away from the
truth, and be turned aside to fables. But you be watch-
ful in all things, endure afflictions, do the work of an
evangelist, fulfill our ministry. For I am already being

> "Something begins inside us in the midst of trials and suffering... we become more like Jesus."

poured out as a drink offering and the time of my departure is at hand.   I have fought the good fight, I have finished the race, I have kept the faith."

"Finally, there is laid up for me the crown of righteousness, which the Lord, the righteous Judge, will give to me on that Day, and not to me only but also unto all who have loved His appearing."

Living a life of sacrifice and being open to God, others and change caused Paul to finish the race and to prepare Timothy for his race.

Questions

1. Is your heart open or closed to God because of trials? _____

    _____

    _____

2. Are you open to others who have learned by being sacrificial leaders? _____

    _____

    _____

3. Live your life for Him and you will find life! Will you? _____

    _____

    _____

    _____

$\mathcal{S}$ STANDS FOR SUFFERING

As a sacrificial leader for Jesus, we are called to suffer.

"Many years and many hurts later, I've come to learn that there are lessons in life that can only be learned through God's curriculum of pain. That's part of what Jesus was getting at in John 15:2 when He told His disciples that every branch that does not bear fruit He prunes so that it will be even more fruitful."[82]

As we go through pruning, we become more fruitful. We can join the great sacrificial leader, the Lord Jesus Christ, in His suffering. If we are godly leaders, we will suffer persecution.

"Suffering: the Cross – the Passion of the Christ – was at the same time both the most horrendous and the most loving act of human history. The only perfect man died instead of all the other people who deserved it. Scripture reminds us that we'll suffer as well: "Yes, and all who desire to live godly in Christ Jesus will suffer persecution." (II Timothy 3:12) "In this world you will have trouble." (John 16:33). "To this you were called, because Christ suffered for you, leaving you an example that you should follow in his steps." (I Peter 2:21) "Notice we do not somehow supplement Christ's suffering. Instead, we join him in suffering in our obedience."[83]

This next statement sums it up well:

> "What is our culture's mantra? Victory without sacrifice, achievement without vision, and get it now and pay later. Yet Paul's simple exhortation rings out over the centuries: 'Endure hardship with us like a good soldier of Christ Jesus.' (II Timothy 2:3)"[84]

Suffering with Him, not for Him

In Romans 8:17, 18 it states,

> *"...and if children then heirs – heirs of God and joint heirs with Christ, if indeed we suffer with Him, that we may also be glorified together. For I consider that the sufferings of this present time are not worthy to be compared with the glory which shall be revealed in us."*

If we suffer with Him, we will be glorified together. The sufferings of this present time are not worthy to be compared to the glory that will be revealed in us!

As we bear the reproach of Christ, we draw closer to Him.

1 Peter 4:14 says,

> *"If you are reproached for the name of Christ, blessed are you, for the Spirit of glory and of God rests upon you. On their part, He is blasphemed, but on your part He is glorified."*

As we bear the reproach of Christ, we draw closer to Him.

I believe there is a special Spirit of Glory and God that is released upon us in a reproach or persecution. As we fellowship with His sufferings, we are broken, humble and tender with those who are going through His trials.

Questions

1. Are you suffering? Is it working for you? _____ How? _____

   _____

   _____

   _____

2. What experience of suffering has tenderized your heart toward others? _____

   _____

   _____

   _____

   _____

   _____

   _____

3. How has God spoken to you in your suffering? _____

   _____

   _____

   _____

I believe there is a special Spirit of Glory and God that is released upon us in a reproach or persecution.

T STANDS FOR TRAINING

Be a lifelong learner

Sacrificial leadership should be a lifelong teacher. We can be trained in the School of Sacrifice. We all need to be lifelong students. As a servant leader in the School of Sacrificial Leadership, we learn about God, life, and others.

Matthew 5:10-12 says,

> *"Blessed are you when they revile and persecute you, and say all kinds of evil against you falsely for My sake. Rejoice and be exceedingly glad, for great is your reward in heaven, for so they persecuted the prophets who were before you."*

We go to the training school of Jesus and the prophets when we are persecuted, reviled and when people say evil things against us. We are told to rejoice. We are tried; we are blessed. We are told ours is the Kingdom of Heaven and great is our reward in heaven.

Be a river not a pond

A pond is stagnant. A river flows with life. Christ's suffering and glorification opened up the river of His life to flow to us. Revelation 22:1-5 tell us:

"And he showed me a pure river of water of life, clear as crystal, proceeding from the throne of God and of the Lamb. In the middle of its street, and on either side of the river, was the tree of life, which bore twelve fruits, each tree yielding its fruit every month. The leaves of the tree were for the healing of the nations. And there shall be no more curse, but the throne of God and the Lamb shall be in it, and His servants shall serve Him. They shall see His face, and His name shall be on their foreheads. There shall be no night there. They need no lamp nor light of the sun, for the Lord God gives them life. And they shall reign forever and ever."

River of life

As we allow His river of life to flow out of us, healing flows to the nations. As we study about sacrifice and experience sacrifice, God can use us in greater ways.

Philippians 3:10, 11 says,

"...that I may know Him and the power of His resurrection, and the fellowship of His sufferings, being conformed to His death, if, by any means, I may attain to the resurrection from the dead."

One man said this in relation to this passage:

> "How could Paul honestly write that? I was a college student when I felt the joy of serving Christ; I certainly wasn't interested in knowing much about suffering. Two decades later my wife and I sat together at a Good Friday service in the church we were attending at the time. I had recently resigned from the church where I had been the pastor. I was out of the pastorate. Suzanne and I were still in shock from the pain and disillusionment of the past two years. Worshiping in that Good Friday service, I suddenly began to understand the previously confounding words of the apostle Paul. Out of my suffering for the sake of Christ came a degree of understanding of the suffering he endured to accomplish my salvation. I couldn't escape the thought that if Jesus had suffered that much for me, didn't he have the right to ask me to share in that suffering?"[85]

> *Life can flow out of the suffering we have experienced in our lives.*

Life flows out of suffering

Life can flow out of the suffering we have experienced in our lives. Sacrificial leadership is very important to Christian servant leadership. The sacrifice is worth the reward of pleasing God and affecting others.

Questions

1. How have you fellowshipped with Christ's sufferings? _____

    _____

    _____

    _____

    _____

    _____

    _____

2. Have you allowed hurts to make you a pond instead of a river? _____

    _____

    _____

    _____

    _____

    _____

    _____

    Let Him pour His life-giving water into your heart!

3. How are you committed to be a lifelong learner in the School of Sacrifice? _____

    _____

    _____

    _____

    _____

Chapter Seven

STRENGTHENING LEADERSHIP

As servant leaders, part of our ministry is strengthening leadership (which I see as when to be a strong leader).

II Corinthians 12:10 states what the Apostle Paul said,

> "*Therefore I take pleasure in infirmities, in reproaches, in needs, in persecutions, in distresses, for Christ's sake. For when I am weak, then I am strong.*"

At times Jesus was a strong leader or a strengthened leader. At times Paul was a strengthened or strong leader. Again, here is another paradox, "When I am weak, then I am strong." I will use the acrostic W-E-A-K for strengthening leadership as we look at where we need to be a strong leader. It appears that Jesus was strong as a leader when the mission the Father had given Him to do was attacked or challenged.

W STANDS FOR WORK WITH GOD

In working with God it is most important to do His will.

It was written of Jesus in Hebrews 10:7,

> "*…then I said, 'Behold, I have come – In the volume of the book it is written of Me – To do Your will, O God.'*"

It appears that Jesus was strong as a leader when the mission the Father had given Him to do was attacked or challenged.

Jesus delighted to do the will of the Father. As a matter of fact, in John 17:4, it says,

> *"I have glorified You on earth, I have finished the work which You have given Me to do."*

Jesus finished the work the Father gave Him to do … He is an example to help us finish the work God has given us to do now.

C.S. Lewis wrote,

> "There are only two kinds of people in the end; those who say to God, 'Thy will be done' and those to whom God says in the end, 'thy will be done.'"[86]

Working with God causes us to do His will on earth as it is in heaven.

What is best for all?

Sometimes leaders need to stick to strong convictions. We will have to make decisions for what is best for all, not for just one or a few. We will need God's guidance to help. We must know God's heart and God's Word, on which we must base our decisions. In Acts 15 it tells how the church leaders decided in Jerusalem what the Gentiles should do as Christians. They did what seemed good to the Holy Spirit and to them.

Prayer is imperative in decision making. Prayer helps our heart to be right before God. Before we need to make a major decision, it is vital to get alone with God and prepare our heart before Him.

E STANDS FOR EXHIBIT STRONG LEADERSHIP

Leaders often have to make tough calls. Why do we do that? Because God has called us to be servant leaders. How can we go about preparing ourselves?

Make a tough call

1. Prepare in Prayer – grow your heart and mind to God and His will.

2. Give yourself a deadline. When do you need to know?

3. Always get wise counsel.

4. Make sure systems are in place to back up a tough decision.

5. Check your emotions. How are you feeling?

Be a servant

"A servant-leader sees his role differently than does a traditional, top-down dictatorial leader. The servant is present to make the worker successful, not vice versa. My workers/employees are not hired to serve

Prayer is imperative in decision making.

me, but to serve the mission of the organization. My role as leader is to facilitate their effectiveness any way I can, much like a coach tries to get optimum performance out of the team players."[87]

Jesus was a strong leader when it came to the mission the Father had given Him to do. Jesus dealt strongly when people tried to take Him or others away from the work God had given them to do.

In Mark's gospel (8:27-32) when Peter said Jesus was not going to the Cross, Jesus replied,

"Get thee behind Me, Satan!"

Jesus was unwavering when it came to staying the course of His mission. We must be strong about the mission God has given each of us to do.

"Servant leaders are accountable to keep the team focused on their goal. Jesus modeled this for those in the school of servant leadership as He taught His disciples the true nature of His mission."[88]

Making the difficult decisions will build your character and develop your leadership skills.

𝒶 STANDS FOR ASSESS THE SITUATION

Tough calls are tough!

Remember tough calls are tough! There are many hard decisions in life.

> "The central task of leadership is influencing God's people toward God's purposes."[89]

It is often difficult to keep people on track. Frequently people covet their old ways in times of change.

> "If pressure is taken off, people will revert to old behavior. Keep people focused on maintaining the change and managing the journey."[90]

Sometimes as a leader a little pressure is needed to focus people. A tough decision is tough. Some people will not like it; others will embrace it.

Expect criticism

One of the challenges of leadership is the criticism you might face in your ministry.

J. Robert Clinton talks about the principle of leadership backlash in Christian leadership.

A tough decision is tough. Some people will not like it; others will embrace it.

"The leadership backlash process item refers to the negative reactions of followers, other leaders within the group, and Christians outside the group to a course of action taken by the leader once ramifications develop from his decision.

It is helpful to recognize the normal pattern:

1. The leader gets a vision (direction) from God.

2. The followers are convinced of the direction.

3. The group moves in the direction given.

4. The group experiences persecution, hard times or attacks from Satan – spiritual warfare is common.

5. There is backlash from the group.

6. The leader is driven to God to seek affirmation in spite of the action's ramifications.

7. God reveals Himself further: who He is, what He intends to do. He makes it clear that He will deliver.

8. God vindicates Himself and the leader.

Leadership backlash tests a leader's perseverance, clarity of vision, and faith."[91]

Part of being a leader is to expect upheaval and learn from it. Backlash happens! Be prepared for criticism.

> *Part of being a leader is to expect upheaval and learn from it.*

Decisions can be costly

Tough decisions are often costly. What will it cost you?
No matter what it costs to make a tough decision, God will
help you. Jesus made this most clear.

> "Jesus was very clear about the cost of discipleship.
> He risked losing large numbers in order to keep
> those who trusted Him and His mission. Jesus be-
> gan equipping those who followed Him by holding
> up high standards of discipleship. As a leader who
> follows Jesus' example, you should make the cost of
> service to others very clear."[92]

Being a leader can cost loneliness, misunderstanding,
rejection, betrayal and many other types of problems. It is
important to count the cost and know what you are to do
and to be as a leader.

Tough decisions often take us to the next level

Many people I know can mark tough decisions that
changed the course of their lives and the lives of others.

> "Crisis process items are those special intense pres-
> sures in human situations that are used by God to test
> and teach dependence on Him. A life-crisis process
> item refers to a crisis characterized by intense pres-
> sure in which the meaning and purpose of life are

searched out, with a result that the leader has experienced God in a new way as the source of life, the sustenance of life and the focus of life."[93]

Making tough decisions causes you to depend on God. You need to trust your judgment and be sure to be motivated by love.

It is very valuable as a leader to know who you are... it is also valuable to know who you are not!

K STANDS FOR KNOW YOUR CALL

It is very valuable as a leader to know who you are! It is helpful to know your calling, your gifts, your personality, your leadership style, your beliefs and the like. The more you know yourself, the better able you are to do what God has called you to do with Him. John the Baptist knew Jesus was the Messiah. He knew he (John) was the voice of one crying in the wilderness. In knowing who he was, he could stay the course.

It is also valuable to know who you are not! It is helpful to know what you are not called to do, what gifts you do not have, what leadership skills you lack and what your weaknesses are in any given areas.

"If a truth-teller says that you are not a good listener, then, what a wonderful thing to come in front of that team and share that, 'So-and-so was kind enough to share feedback with me about my listening. I didn't realize that when you would say things to me, I would jump right on to my own agenda. But now I know and I would like to improve it, and the way I can improve it is if you will help me.'"[94]

When we know who we are not or what we need to do to improve as in "good listening," a team can help us grow. When we know our gifts and strengths, we will know who can help us with our weaknesses as a servant leader.

Follow Jesus and biblical examples

In strengthening leadership skills (strong leadership), it is important to follow Jesus and good biblical examples. In our attitudes we need to follow Jesus and good biblical examples.

John 12:26 says,

> *"If anyone serves Me, let him follow Me, and where I am, there My servant will be also. If anyone serves Me, him My Father will honor."*

In I Corinthians 11:1, Paul says,

> *"Imitate me, just as I also imitate Christ."*

Paul said to imitate or do what I do as I do what Jesus is doing! Paul goes on in Ephesians 5:1, 2 to state,

> *"Therefore be imitators of God as dear children. And walk in love, as Christ also has loved us and given*

Himself for us, an offering and a sacrifice to God for a sweet-smelling aroma."

We have to follow Jesus as we walk in love as servant leaders.

One of the secrets to strengthening leadership skills and attitudes is found in II Corinthians 12:9, 10, when Paul wanted the thorn in his flesh to be removed, and the Lord answered him,

> *"And He said to me, 'My grace is sufficient for you, for My strength is made perfect in weakness.' Therefore most gladly I will rather boast in my infirmities, that the power of Christ may rest upon me. Therefore I take pleasure in infirmities, in reproaches, in needs, in persecutions, in distresses, for Christ's sake. For when I am weak, then I am strong."*

Christian servant leadership brings us to hard decisions and places. This develops character and broadens our ministry. There are many attitudes needed during tough calls: humility, grace, honesty, integrity, vulnerability, listening, and the like. May the attitudes of Jesus become more and more ours.

> "May the attitudes of Jesus become more and more our own."

Questions

1. Do you have a tough call to make? _____

    _____

    _____

    _____

    _____

    _____

2. Is it hard for you to make a tough call? Why?

    _____

    _____

    _____

    _____

3. What are your weaknesses where His strength will be made perfect? _____

    _____

    _____

    _____

    _____

    _____

    _____

Conclusion

I love what Ken Blanchard and Phil Hodges said,

"Leadership is not something you do to people; it's something you do with people."[95]

I would also like to say servant leadership is not something you do for God, but rather it is something you do with God. It is something that should be done right and with a right attitude. My hope is that you will pour out into others the skills you have learned in this workbook.

More questions

1. What are the main things you learned?_____

    _____

    _____

    _____

    _____

    _____

    _____

    _____

    _____

    _____

2. What are you going to do with what you have learned?_____

    _____

    _____

    _____

    _____

    _____

    _____

    _____

ENDNOTES

Introduction

1   Spears, Larry C. and Lawrence, Michele, *Focus on Leadership*, John Wiley & Sons, Inc., New York, NY
©2002, p. 3

2   Ibid., p. 1.

3   Ibid., p. 13

4   Ibid., p. 16

5   Blanchard, Ken and Hodges, Phil, *Lead Like Jesus*,
W. Publishing Group, ©2005, p. 4

6   Ibid., p. xiii

Chapter One

7   Spears, Larry, *Focus on Leadership*, John Wiley & Sons, Inc.,
©2002, pp. 5-8

8   Blanchard, Ken, and Hodges, Phil, *The Servant Leader*,
J. Countryman, Nashville, TN ©2003, p 22

9   Ibid., p. 24

10   Ibid., pp. 50-57

11   John 13:1-17, NKJV

12   Thrall, Bill, McNicol, Bruce, McElrath, Ian, *The Ascent
of a Leader*, San Francisco, CA, Josey-Bass A Wiley
Company, 1999, pp. 114-115

13   Spears, Larry C., *Focus on Leadership*, John Wiley & Sons,
The Greenleaf Center for Servant Leadership, ©2002, p. 5

14   Ephesians 4:11-16

15   Kenneth Wuest, *Word Studies in the Greek New Testament,
Vol. I*, Wm. B. Eerdmans Publishing
Company, Grand Rapids, MI 1973, p. 101

16   *New Spirit Filled Life*, New King James Version, edited
by Jack Hayford, Thomas Nelson, Inc., Nashville, TN
©2002, p. 1651

17   Blanchard, Ken, and Hodges, Phil, *The Servant Leader*, J.
Countryman, Nashville, TN ©2003 p. 20

18   Romans 12:9-21

19   Rowe, W. Glenn, and Guerrero, Laura, *Cases in Leadership*, Sage Publishing, Inc., Thousand Oaks, CA © 2011, p. 282

20   James 5:15

21   Rowe, W. Glenn, and Guerrero, Laura, *Cases in Leadership*, p. 287

22   Silk, Danny, *Culture of Honor*, Destiny Image Publishers, Inc., Shippensburg, PA © 2009, p. 25

23   Hebrews 10:23-25

24   Rowe and Guerrero, *Cases in Leadership*, pp. 284-285

25   Ephesians 4:15, 16

26   Clinton, J. Robert, *The Making of a Leader,* NavPress, Colorado Springs, CO ©1985, p. 58

27   II Peter 1:5-8

28   Acts 1:1-3

29   Rowe and Guerrero, *Cases in Leadership*, p. 81

30   Ibid., p. 82

Chapter Two

31   Wilkerson, David, *The Cross and the Switchblade*, The Berkeley Publishing Co., a division of Penguin Putnam, Inc., New York, NY 1962

32   *Webster's Pocket Dictionary*, Trident Press International, Quebecor, Peru. 2002

33   Wagner, C. Peter, *Acts of the Holy Spirit*, Regal Books, Ventura, CA © 2000, p. 495

34   Silk, Danny, *Culture of Honor*, Destiny Image Publishing, Inc. Shippensburg, PA © 2009, p. 29

35   McNeal, Reggie, *Revolution in Leadership*, Abingdon Press, Nashville, TN, 1998 p. 32

36   Ibid., pp. 39-42

37   Adams, Michael, *Promoted from Leader to Servant*, Heart of Heaven Ministries, © 2009 by Michael Adams, p. 93

38   Ibid., p. 146

Chapter Three

39   Rowe & Guerrero, *Cases in Leadership*, p. 345

40   Blanchard & Hodges, *Lead Like Jesus*, p. 84

41   Phillips, Tom, *Leaders on Leadership*, edited by George Barna, Ventura CA 1997 p. 233

42   Taken from Rick Kingham's Notes in a Northwest Graduate University Course on Leadership in September, 2000

43   Hackman, Michael Z., and Johnson, Craig E., Leadership: *A Communication Perspective*, Loveland Press, Inc., Long Grove, IL © 2004 p. 358

44   Block, Peter, *Stewardship*, Berett-Koehler Publishers, San Francisco, CA © 1998, 1996, p. 234

45   Rowe & Guerrero, *Cases in Leadership*, p. 205

46   Hackman and Johnson, *Leaders: A Communication Perspective*, p. 206

47   Matthew 16:21-23

48   Barna, George, *Leaders on Leadership*, Regal Books, Ventura, CA 1997 p. 58

49   Blanchard and Hodges, *The Servant Leader*, p. 122

Chapter Four

50   Anderson. Dr. Lynn, *They Smell Like Sheep*, Howard Publishing Co., West Monroe, LA 1997, p. 4

51   Keller, Phillip, *A Shepherd looks at Psalm 23*, Zondervan Publishing House, Grand Rapids, MI, 1970, p. 116

52   Clinton, Dr. J. Robert, *The Making of a Leader*, p. 90

53   Ibid, p. 92

54   Blanchard and Hodges, *Lead Like Jesus*, p. 31-32

55   Herron, Michael J., *Heart of a Psalmist*, Latter Glory Publishing, Moses Lake, WA © 2010, p. 66

56   Clinton, Dr. J. Robert, *The Making of a Leader*, p. 58

57   Ibid., p. 58, 59

58   Leighton Ford, *Leaders on Leadership*, George Barna Editor, Regal Books, Ventura, CA 1997, p. 141

59   Ibid., p. 141

60   Block, Peter, *Stewardship*, p. 36

61   Hackman and Johnson, *Leadership*, p. 58

62   Ford, Leighton, *Leaders on Leadership*, p. 121

63   Pocket Dictionary,

64   Kreider, Larry, *21 Tests of Effective Leadership*, Destiny Image Publishers, Inc., Shippensburg, PA © 2010, p. 156

65   Guiness, Os, *The Call*, W Publishing Group, Nashville, TN © 2003, p. 105

66   Anderson, Dr. Lynn, *They Smell Like Sheep*, p. 4

Chapter Five

67   Rowe, and Guererro, *Cases in Leadership*, p. 133

68   Ibid., pp. 234-235

69   Hackman and Johnson, *Leadership*, p. 64

70   Anderson, Leith, *Leadership that Works*, Bethany Publishing House, Minneapolis, MN © 1999, p. 33

71   Blanchard and Hodges, *The Servant Leader*, p. 64

72   Kreider, Larry, *21 Tests of Effective Leadership*, Destiny Images Publisher, Shippensburg, PA, © 2010, p. 94

73   Thrall, Bill, McNicol, Bruce and McElrath, *The Ascent of a Leader*, Jowey-Bass A Wiley Company, San Francisco, CA 1999, p. 44

74   Kreider, *21 Tests of Effective Leadership*, p. 96

Chapter Six

75   Bonhoeffer, Dietrich *The Cost of Discipleship*, MacMillin Publishing, New York, NY 1937, p. 64

76   Hull, Bill, *The Complete Book of Discipleship*, NavPress, Colorado Spring, CO, © 2006, p. 108

77   Maxwell, John, *The 21 Irrefutable Laws of Leadership*, Thomas Nelson Publishers, Nashville, TN 1998, p. 183

78   Ibid., p. 188

79   Krieder, Larry, 21 *Tests of Effective Leadership*, p. 188

80   Adams, Michael, *Promoted from Leader to Servant*, p. 142

81   DePree, Max, *Focus on Leadership*, John Wiley & Sons, Inc., New York, NY 2002, p. 95

82   Preston, Gary, *Character Forged from Conflict*, Bethany House Publishers, Minneapolis, MN 1999 p. 147

83   Hull, Bill, *The Complete Book of Discipleship*, NavPress, Colorado Springs, CO 2006, p. 151

84   Ibid., p. 283

85   Preston, Gary D., *Character Forged in Conflict*, p. 42

Chapter Seven

86   Thrall, Bill, *The Ascent of a Leader*, p. 180 87 Finzel, Hans, *Leaders on Leadership*, Regal Books, Ventura, CA 1997, p. 273-274

88   Wilkes, C. Gene, *Jesus on Leadership*, Life Way Press, Nashville, TN © 2009, p. 115

89   Clinton, Dr. J. Robert, *The Making of a Leader*, p. 203

90   Blanchard & Hodges, *The Servant Leader*, p. 67

91   Clinton, Dr. J. Robert, *The Making of a Leader*, p. 109

92   Wilkes, C. Gene, *Jesus on Leadership*, p. 91

93   Clinton, Dr. J. Robert, *The Making of a Leader*, p. 164-165

94   Blanchard, *The Servant Leader*, p. 104

95   Blanchard & Hodges, *The Servant Leader*, p. 113

96   Wimber, John, *Signs and Wonders and Church Growth*, Vineyard Ministries International, Anaheim, CA ©1987

BIBLIOGRAPHY

Adams, Michael, *Promoted from Leader to Servant*, USA ©2009, Heart of Heaven Ministries

Agosto, Ephraim, *Servant Leadership: Jesus and Paul*, Article by Ronald Brown.

Allen, Roland, *The Spontaneous Expansion of the Church*, Wipf & Stock Publishers, Eugene, OR ©1962

Bakke, Ray, *A Theology as Big as a City*, Downers Grove, IL, InterVarsity Press, ©1997.

Barna, George, *Leaders on Leadership*, Ventura CA, Regal Books, ©1997.

Barnes, Grace Preedy, *Servant First*, Indianapolis, IN, Precedent Press, ©2006.

Bennis, Warren, *On Becoming a Leader*, Cambridge, MA, Perseus Books, ©1989.

Blanchard, Ken and Hodges, Phil, *Lead Like Jesus,* W. Publishing Group, Nashville, TN ©2005.

Bosch, David J., *Transforming Mission*, Orbis Books, Maryknoll, NY ©2003

Clinton, Dr. J. Robert, *The Making of a Leader*, Colorado Springs, CO, Navepress, ©1988.

Cooke, Graham, *Coming into Alignment*, Brilliant Book House, Vacaville, CA ©2009

Cooke, Graham, *Developing Your Prophetic Gifting*, Kent, Sovereign World Ltd., England, ©1994

Cooke, Graham, *Qualities of a Spiritual Warrior*, Brilliant Book House, Vacaville, CA ©2008

Covey, Steven R., *The 8th Habit from Effectiveness to Greatness*, New York, NY, Free Press, ©2004.

Drucker, Peter F., *Managing the Non-Profit Organization*, New York, NY, Harper Business, ©1990

Erwin, Gayle D., *The Jesus Style*, Dallas, TX, Word Publishing, ©1983, 1988.

Finzel, Hans, *The Top Ten Mistakes Leaders Make*, Colorado Spring, CO, David C. Cook Publishing Co., ©2007.

Foster, Richard J., *Celebration of Discipleship*, San Francisco, CA, Harper Collins Publisher, ©1988.

Frick, Don M., *Servant Leadership Primer*, Source: Bing on Internet.

Greenleaf, Robert K., *Servant Leadership*, New York/Mahuch, NJ, Paulist Press, ©1988.

Guisness, Os, *The Call*, Nashville, TN, W. Publishing Group, ©1998, 2003.

Hackman, Michael Z., and Johnson, Craig E., *Leadership: A Communication Perspective*, Long Grove, IL, Waveland Press, Inc., ©2004.

Hayes, John B., *Sub-merge*, Ventura, CA, Regal Books, ©2006

Herron, J. Michael, *Heart of a Psalmist*, Latter Glory Publishing, Moses Lake, WA, ©2010

Hetland, Leif, *Soaring Like Eagles*, Killen, AL, Leif Hetland Ministries, ©2006.

Hybels, Bill, *Courageous Leadership*, Grand Rapids, MI, Zondervan Publishing Company, ©2002

Images of Servant Leadership, America, NY, October 2006, Vol. 195, Issue 11, p. 39 [1 page].

Irving, Justin A., *Servant Leadership and the Effectiveness of Teams, Doctorate of Philosophy and Organizational Leadership*, March, ©2005.

Johnson, Bill, *The Supernatural Power of a Transformed Mind*, Destiny Image Publishers, Inc., Shippensburg, PA ©2005

Johnson, Bill, *When Heaven Invades Earth*, Destiny Image Publishers, Inc., Shippensburg, PA ©2003

New King James Version, ©1982 by Thomas Nelson, Inc. Used by permission. All rights reserved.

Kreider, Larry, *Authentic Spiritual Mentoring*, Ventura, CA, Regal Books, ©2008

Kreider, Larry, *Building Your Personal House of Prayer*, Destiny Image Publishers, Inc., Shippensburg, PA ©2008

Kreider, Larry, *21 Tests of Effective Leadership*, Shippensburg, PA, Destiny Image Publishers, Inc., ©2010.

Levanduski, Stan, *Advantages of Leadership*, April 22, 2008 Taken from the Internet.

Maxwell, John, *The 21 Irrefutable Laws of Leadership*, Nashville, TN, Thomas Nelson Publishers, ©1998.

Maxwell, John, *The 17 Indisputable Laws of Teamwork*, Nashville, TN, Thomas Nelson Publishers, ©2004.

McIntosh, Gary L., and Rima, Samuel D., *Overcoming the Dark Side of Leadership*, Grand Rapids, MI, Baker Books, ©1997.

McKenna, Robert, Ph.D, *Dying to Lead*, Seattle, WA, USA, Xulon Press, ©2008.

Merrill, Jr., Daryl, Dr., *Teams that Work*, Niles, IL, Mall Publishing Co., ©2003

Miller, Calvin, *The Empowered Leader*, Nashville, TN, Broadman & Holman Publishing, ©1995

Morris, Linus J., *The High Impact Church*, Christian Associates International, ©1998

New Spirit Filled Life Bible, Thomas Nelson Publishing Co., ©2002. Used by permission. All rights reserved.

Ogne, Steven and Tibbott, Neil, *Empowering Leaders*, Seattle, WA, Class Notes from Bakke Graduate University ©2004.

Parish, Fawn, *Honor*, Renew Books, Ventura, CA ©1999

Pierce, Chuck, and Systema, Rebecca Wagner *Possessing Your Inheritance*, Renew Books, Ventura, CA ©1999

Pierce, Chuck, *Redeeming the Time*, Charisma House, Lake Mary FL, ©2009

Preston, Gary, Character *Forged from Conflict*, Bethany House Publishers, Minneapolis, MN, ©1999

Rowe, Glenn, and Guerrero, Laura, *Cases in Leadership*, Sage Publications, Thousand Oaks, CA ©2011

Schaeffer, Francis A., *Character of Servant Leadership*, Institute of Church Leadership Development, Presentation, ©2003.

Sheets, Dutch, *Intercessory Prayer*, Regal Publishing, Ventura, CA ©1996

Spears, Larry, *Practicing Servant Leadership*, Fall 2004, issue 34, Leader to Leader Institute Journal.

Stanley, Andy, *Visioneering*, Sister, OR, Multnomah Publishers, ©1999.

Thrall, Bill, McNicol, Bruce, McElrath, Ken, *The Ascent of a Leaders*, San Francisco, CA, Josey-Bass A Wiley Company, ©1999.

Van Gelder, Craig, *The Essence of the Church*, Baker Books, Grand Rapids, MI, ©2002

Wagner, Dr. C. Peter, *Acts of the Holy Spirit,* Regal Books, Ventura, CA ©2000

Wagner, Dr. C. Peter, *Apostles of the City*, Wagner Publications, Colorado Spring, CO, ©2000

Whitmore, John, *Coaching for Performance*, London, England, Nicholas Brealey, ©2002

Wilkes, C. Gene, *Jesus on Leadership*, Nashville, TN 1996, Life Way Press, 10th Reprint ©2009.

Wimber, John, *Power Evangelism*, Hodder and Stroughton, London, England, ©1985

Wimber, John, *Signs and Wonders and Church Growth*, Vineyard Ministries International, Anaheim, CA ©1987

About the Author

Pastor Dan C. Hammer is a true servant-leader and visionary with a passion to reach the unloved with the Gospel of Jesus Christ. Dan is committed to intercessory prayer and uncovering the gifts of the Holy Spirit in the lives of believers. He regularly teaches how to attain life's full potential by understanding God's purpose for your life. Know your gifts, know your purpose!

Recognized as an apostle and member of the International Coalition of Apostles, Dan has traveled the world helping plant and develop churches, schools and orphanages in many nations including Mexico, India, South Africa, Uganda, Cuba, Turkey, Italy, Israel, Thailand, Fiji, Poland and Russia.

Dan is the state coordinator for the United States Apostolic Alliance with Dutch Sheets. He holds a Doctoral Degree of Ministry at Bakke Graduate University. He is on staff at Seattle Bible College and serves as ongoing advisor for Aglow International. Dan is the Chancellor by appointment of Dr. C. Peter Wagner at Wagner Leadership Institute-Seattle Campus where he holds a Doctor of Practical Ministry diploma.

Dan co-founded the Northwest New Wine Network, a monthly regional gathering of pastors, intercessors and leaders. This September Dan will co-launch a new school with his son, John Hammer at Sonrise Christian Center called Sonrise Global Supernatural School of Ministry.

In 1986 Dan and his wife Terry planted Sonrise Christian Center (formerly Sonrise Chapel) as an independent Fellowship of Christian Assemblies in Everett, Washington where they continue to serve as senior pastors.

They have three adult children and four grandchildren and reside in the beautiful Pacific Northwest.

CPSIA information can be obtained at www.ICGtesting.com
Printed in the USA
BVOW032048230512

290589BV00004B/1/P